Women in rural development
Critical issues

Women
in rural development
Critical issues

International Labour Office   Geneva

ISBN 92-2-102388-5

First published 1980
Third impression 1984

HN
980
.W 65
cap. 2

Printed in Switzerland

Direct   21 Ja 86   Econ. + mgt.

Table of contents

ACKNOWLEDGEMENTS

The cover photographs are from the ILO Photo Library, Geneva.
They illustrate rural women working at land-tilling, transport,
road construction and jar-making in Burundi, Haiti, India and
Dahomey.

I. PREFACE

The World Employment Conference in June 1976 noted that
women constitute the group at the bottom of the ladder in many
developing countries, in respect of employment, poverty, education,
training and status.   Concerning rural women, the Conference
recommended that measures be taken to relieve their work burden
and drudgery by improving working and living conditions,
as well as by providing more resources for investment.   The
Programme on Rural Women, which is part of the ILO's World
Employment Programme, attempts to translate this recommendation
into action.   In view of the inadequate research done on employment patterns and problems of rural women, the main focus of
the Programme has been on studies and field research subcontracted
to researchers and policy makers in Third World countries.   The
general approach of the Programme is to gradually move from a
solid information base to the dissemination and exchange of such
information through seminars and workshops, followed by the
planning and implementation of technical co-operation projects
in close consultation, where possible, with rural women's own
organisations.

In May 1978, with assistance from the Dutch Ministry of
Foreign Affairs, the ILO's Rural Employment Policies Branch
invited a number of specialists to Geneva to participate in
a consultation on the subject of Women and Rural Development.
The purpose of this consultation was two-fold: (a) to
establish communication with people familiar with the area
of women and rural development, with the purpose of defining
the most pressing areas for research, policy, and action;
and (b) to make the ILO's work better known to individuals and
institutions concerned with rural women in the Third World.

Participants from different regions were invited and
several observers were also present.   They were asked to make
short presentations based on their research and related to
the following general topics: modes of production, agrarian
structures, and women's work; sex roles and the division of
labour in rural economies; effects of the penetration of
the market on rural women; and, rural development and women.
More specifically, participants were asked to derive conclusions
from their work and experience that could be relevant to
programmes on rural women.

This booklet includes a selection of abstracts, written
by the participants themselves.   The views expressed are
those of the participants and not necessarily of the ILO;
they outline the main issues as seen and presented by the
participants. A list of the main issues raised in the discussion
that developed at each session is included, together with the
conclusions that followed.

We wish to share these results with a broader audience, in
the belief that they may contribute to other programmes concerned
with rural women and with rural development in general.

Dharam Ghai,
and
Zubeida Ahmad
Rural Employment Policies Branch,
Employment and Development Department.

A. MODES OF PRODUCTION, AGRARIAN
   STRUCTURES AND WOMEN'S WORK

Rural women in Yugoslavia

Ruža First-Dilić

The objective of my talk is to describe the present situation
of the female labour force in agriculture in the Socialist Federated
Republic of Yugoslavia.   The evaluation of working relations
between the sexes covers both sectors of agriculture;   the socialist
sector - which includes only about 14 per cent of a total of some
10 million hectares of arable land - and the private, peasant
farming sector - which comprises about 86 per cent of the total
arable land, and is cultivated by 2.6 million peasant families, each
holding an average of 3.5 hectares of arable land.

The prevalence of smallholdings requires different forms of
organising production, so as to promote a faster and more effective
development of agriculture;   for the majority of peasant family
farms, production is based on traditional work patterns, even when
modern farm technology is provided.   Socialist farms supplied with
modern means of production - co-operatives, agro-enterprises, etc. -
have not introduced significant changes in productive relations.
In both production modes, women are still relegated to a marginal
social position, as substitutes for men working off the farm.

In what follows I will summarise the existing situation of
women in the agricultural labour force.   The analysis is based on
comparative statistical data from the Agricultural Censuses of 1948,
1953, 1961 and 1969.   Several issues could be delineated.

First, women provide a substitute agricultural labour force on
both co-operative, i.e. socialist, and private farms.   They take
over the work left by men who have moved out of agriculture.   As
a rule this work is associated with the lowest qualifications and
is rewarded with the lowest income levels.   Further, it is work
without prestige.   None the less, farm women have no alternative
other than the agricultural profession: employment in agriculture
is for them a social and economic necessity rather than a result of
their own free choice.

Second, women now represent the majority of the agricultural
labour force, that is, the work force in agriculture has been
feminised.   However, this feminisation seems to be a temporary
phenomenon, generated by the unequal intersectoral demands for male
and female labour.   It tends to occur in the early phases of
industrialisation and/or in regions undergoing rapid industrial
change.

Several indicators show that the future trend in the sex ratio
of the agricultural labour force will be towards a reduction of
female labour participation.   The most obvious one is that the
rate of farm girls completing eight years of compulsory education
is equalising with that of farm boys.   In addition, their enrol-
ment in high school and vocational education is also increasing.

This implies that rural girls and women are gaining the formal basis for vocational selection, and that in the future gender may not be the only selective criteria for farming.

It should be stressed here that the recent activity of the extension service centres in rural communities is oriented towards attracting rural women so as to provide them with information on new farm technology and methods. Specialisation of production on farms large enough to turn to market production is also encouraged. Although at present fewer women than men attend these centres - a proportion which does not compare with the sex ratio of the agricultural labour force - those who do will tend to influence their female neighbours by transmitting their new skills and greater knowledge. Social action oriented towards mobilising farm women has been recently initiated, among others through organising clubs for women of co-operatives. Thus, as agriculture gains in status as a socially and politically recognised profession, the rural labour force will tend to become professionally stable. A series of new laws supports this trend.

Third, farm women are bearers of a threefold role. They carry out between 60 to 70 per cent of all the farm work, and are engaged in agricultural production for at least two-thirds of their normal working time. In addition, they do all the household work together with the majority of chores related to raising children. Yet, rural women appear to be an underutilised human resource. If given better technical and social training, they could make a greater contribution both to agricultural and rural development, as well as to the development of society in general. The latter point should be particularly emphasised since in such overworked and limited living conditions, in addition to being socially isolated in the slowly changing patriarchal rural community, rural women are perceived as not being fully conscious of their status. Yet, we might ask, why do they tend to leave the farm after completing elementary education and why are they increasingly marrying non-farming men, which takes them out of farming.

Thus, we could conclude that rural women in general and farm women in particular in Yugoslavia are conscious of their unequal social position when compared with the social position of urban and/or non-farm women, on the one side, and of rural and/or farm men, on the other. Yet they are still not dealing directly with the problem, but instead trying to change their social position in indirect ways.

A tentative conclusion can be drawn: women in the agricultural labour force in a post-revolutionary, early socialist society, continue to be in a marginal social position, thus representing a neglected resource for agricultural and of rural development. It is a negative consequence resulting from their occupational position in farming, and their specific role in society and the peasant family.[1]

---

[1] More extensive information on the subject can be found in:

First-Dilić, Ruža: Žena - aktivni poljoprivredni proizvodjač
1974   ("Women as active agricultural producers").
                    Žena, Vol. 32, No. 2, pp. 18-26.

First-Dilić, Ruža: Položoj poljoprivrednice u radu i samoupravl-
1974   janju ("Position of farm women in work and self-
                       management"). Marksističke Sveske, Vol. 4,
                       Nos. 1/4, pp. 313-326.

First-Dilić, Ruža: Sex roles in rural Yugoslavia. The International
1974   Journal of Sociology of the Family, Vol. 4,
                       No. 2, pp. 161-169.

First-Dilić, Ruža: Žena u socijalističkom razvoju poljoprivrede
1977   ("Women in the socialist development of agri-
                       culture"). Socijalizam, Vol. 20, Nos. 7/8,
                       pp. 1392-1405.

First-Dilić, Ruža: The productive roles of farm women in Yugoslavia.
1978   Socialogia Ruralis, Nos. 2/3. Forthcoming.

A methodological approach to analysing the effects of capitalist agriculture on women's roles and their position within the community

Kate Young

There seems to be almost universal agreement that one of the commonest effects of development is to relegate women to the sub-sistence sector. Technology, credit and know-how are concentrated in the hands of men while women are assigned the non-modernised, subsistence sector, in other words food production for domestic consumption. I am somewhat concerned by this seemingly common agreement. That is not to say that a common effect of development is not to concentrate modern agricultural machines and implements and new varieties of seed and so on into the hands of men, nor to deny that many of the assumptions that westerners hold about correct gender roles have led to men being exclusively given agricultural training, even in societies in which women are traditionally the farmers. My unease stems from the relegation argument.

It appears to be suggested that the marginalisation of women to food production (sometimes called the feminisation of agriculture) is a world-wide phenomenon. However, my own limited knowledge of the effects of development in Latin America would suggest that this is hardly a sufficient analysis even though it is possible that women are participating to a greater extent now in all phases of produc-tion of food crops than in the past. Rather I would suggest that a common effect of development policies is to make women central to the production of crops destined for the market. This production may either be on a household basis in which case the women work as unpaid labourers for the man/men of the household, or production may be on a much larger scale in which the women provide very cheap seasonal labour for the owners of the enterprise. In this latter case the women may form part of a familial labour group (payment going to the "head of the family"), or member of an all-female work gang (payment going to the gang leader for redistribution to the workers), or be hired as individual labourers.

Women's role in cash crop production may or may not be asso-ciated with an increasing percentage of female labour time also being spent on food production on small household plots. Frequently however, we are looking at labour flows between self-provisioning sectors of the rural economy and the more capitalised sector producing for the market. The insistence in the literature on the pushing of women into subsistence, or their marginalisation as it is often described, may possibly come from an unequal number of studies being carried out in certain parts of the world in which this is in fact an effect of capitalist development in agriculture. On the other hand, it may well stem from our inadequate understanding of rural production systems and the ways in which they have been integrated, and the extent to which they have been integrated, into the market economy. It seems to me that we may well have an inade-quate understanding of the gender specific roles assigned to members of productive units within these rural systems, and indeed of the nature of the productive unit itself. As a part of this, there is often a lack of specification of the place and importance of female roles, how they interlock with, or are functionally complementary to, male roles. Lastly, little is written about the representation of these roles in the system of beliefs and practices stemming from them, in other words, how these roles are represented in ideology and reproduced over time.

Having made this criticism, it is clear that I am bound to be asked what I would consider an adequate analysis of a given production system (and the totality of women's roles within it) which would provide a basis for understanding how it has been modified in the process of integration into the market, and how this in turn has affected inter-gender relations.

Firstly, the nature of the productive system prior to integration must be delineated. All elements of production should be covered including the production of the following generation (not merely childbirth, but also child-care and socialisation). Each of these elements would correspond to what I call for convenience sake (although the concept is clearly problematical) a labour process. Taking each labour process individually, a number of questions about all aspects of control over the means of production have to be posed. For example, is one dealing with formal or real ownership? In other words, is a distinction made between possession and ownership; this is a particularly important point in systems where women are "owners" of land, but in fact social ordinances forbid them working it directly. It is also important to note that ownership of the important element of the means of production, land for example, is not a sufficient condition to ensure that a labour process can be set in motion. In other words, access to a variety of other inputs (also means of production) are essential to carry through the labour process: for example, seeds, fertilizers, water, animal traction, labour. It is common enough in the literature to read of women who have land but lack seed or fertilizer, or having all three lack the ability to command labour to bring the three inputs into working relation. This latter point is one which I think is often insufficiently elaborated in the literature: that is that the sexes often have very different access to various categories of labour - female, male, young, old - even in situations where there is a clear-cut gender allocation of tasks and a high degree of non-substitutability of tasks. Women typically can call upon their young children, or their female relatives; in some areas they may also call upon their brother(s) (but they are constrained by the demands made on their own time by their own familial requirements). When what is needed is male labour, and no kinsmen are about, women may be unable to ensure that a labour process they have set in motion can be carried through. This labour command bottleneck may be resolved where labourers (non-kinsmen) are available for payment in kind and women have access to the necessary resources, for example, millet for beer brewing. Men may be similarly affected when there are tasks within a total labour process which absolutely require female labour; it seems to be quite common that female labour cannot be acquired even for payment in kind.

These are the sorts of constraints that allow demographic hazards (too many sons, too many daughters) to play havoc on the ability of a production unit constituted by a single household to survive under certain conditions of labour shortage.

Lastly, we have to ask who controls the proceeds of each labour process. This can be in terms of rights over distribution within the production unit or beyond it. We may be looking at a system in which the head of a large compound with a number of constituent households (either conjugal couples, or men with several wives) dispenses the totality of the compound's product, or a system in which each unit within the compound is allocated a certain quantity of the produce for consumption according to numbers while

the seed grain for the following year's sowing is zealously guarded
by the compound head; or we may be dealing with a system of peasant
households in which the women are charged with "husbanding" their
household's food supplies throughout the year and also ensuring an
adequate supply of sprouted seed for the next year's planting.
We must beware of a number of assumptions about the distribution
of the proceeds, in particular the common assumption that the household is a unit within which all members have equal access to and
rights over household resources. In fact in many societies social
rules as to the correct way in which the proceeds should be spent
differentiate considerably between males and females; for example,
expenditure of the so-called household budget on cigarettes and
alcohol by men is often paired to strong sanctions against such
consumption by women. Food consumption within the household varies
widely with, in many cases, an age and sex hierarchy operating,
elder males getting the "lion's share" with children next and adult
women last. Expenditures during life-crisis rituals again may
well differ by gender: for example, male circumcision ceremonies
may demand heavy outlays of produce (including the typically male
produce - livestock) while female circumcision, where it takes
place, may require none or a small-scale expenditure of grains
(considered a female product).

Having made such an inventory of labour processes, the next
step must be to attempt to see how they relate to one another and
how they are co-ordinated so as to ensure social reproduction, in
other words, continuance of the system over time. There are clearly
a number of important questions to be asked but in no way is it
possible to produce an exhaustive check list: instead it is probably
more suggestive to indicate areas of questions. Firstly, one
should ask in what way are the distinct labours within labour processes and between labour processes linked? Are they related to
each other in a hierarchical or non-hierarchical way? In other
words, is there a single (or a small number of) key labour processes
upon which the others turn? This should give one an insight into
relations of domination and subordination. In addition, is there
privileged access of one gender to co-ordinating roles? Or to
turn this question on its head, are women excluded from those labour
processes which one has identified as playing a key co-ordinating
role? Lastly, it is essential to analyse how this hierarchy and
the privileged access are represented in other aspects of social
life (political or religious institutions, ideology). This may
give one an insight into how what could be called the concrete
manifestation of an abstract division of labour (and in particular
the sexual division of labour) is internalised and then reproduced
by the participants in actual behaviour and justification of
behaviour. In some cases, this may take the form of an assumption
that the sexual division of labour derives from natural attributes
of men and women (all of us have heard all too often that women are
"naturally" better equipped to do meticulous, time-consuming,
repetitive work and so on). In others, women's subordination is
maintained by a series of repressive measures rather than internalised conceptualisations.

Since the foregoing discussion has been somewhat abstract,
perhaps it would be useful to illustrate the approach from my own
field data from Mexico.

In the nineteenth century in the area where I worked, women
were renowned for their skill as weavers. They acquired raw and
unseeded cotton from local traders (male), which they, with the help

of their children (possibly of both sexes at least while they were young) cleaned, spun and wove lengths of tough cotton cloth. These lengths they then made into skirts and tops for themselves and their daughters, into trousers and blouse-like tops for the men, and shawls for both. Lengths surplus to domestic requirements were bartered locally or sold to the traders. From the traders the women were able to acquire inputs for other labour processes such as metal tools (machetes, plough tips) or oxen, as well as ornaments for the church, dynamite and alcohol for religious festivities. The women controlled the labour process involved, most of the inputs into it, the timing of the totality of the tasks necessary, and the proceeds. From such activity they apparently derived a high standing in their households and in the community. None the less women were barred from the administration of the church although they were absolutely essential participants in the most important rituals of the village and without them the health and safety of the village and all its members could not be ensured. But again, the principal actor in the ritual was the man not his wife. These church rituals provided, I would argue, the dynamic to surplus production (which in poor harvest years ensured adequate provision of subsistence). Women were also barred from participation in the local (i.e. village) government and did not thus have a formal position of effective power in the administration of village affairs. One of the primary concerns of the village government was the allocation of rights in the means of production upon which most of the other labour processes in the village were based: land. Women did not work the land (although they provided labour at peak periods, such as harvest) and even as owners of rights in land, did not have effective posses-sion of it. They did not have effective control over the supply of raw cotton but were dependent for this upon the traders who appear to have been "outsiders" to the areas. This relationship is, in fact, not very clear in that the traders who provided raw cotton may also have appropriated the finished product (i.e. giving space for manipulation of prices to the detriment of the producer).

It could be argued that the basis for the reproduction of the system was in some measure dependent upon the women's activity as weavers. None the less, this key role in society was not repre-sented in the political sphere, rather it was denied. In the religious sphere the necessity for the male-female pair in ritual could be interpreted as a representation in part of the complemen-tarity of productive activity through the exchange of the product for inputs needed in other vital labour processes. As far as co-ordinating roles are concerned, they were exclusively given to males who, for example, appear to have been primarily responsible for non-local exchanges of cotton cloths for other necessary inputs. They were also exclusively involved in the public organisation of the ritual life of the community.

Having established the nature of the productive system and its mechanisms for reproduction, the next task is to analyse the nature of the contradictions set up by the intervention of capital. Clearly, here one has to be able to specify what type of capital is involved: are we looking at mercantile or industrial capital. The importance here is the difference in the ways in which a surplus is extracted from the local system: mercantile capital typically appropriates surplus labour through the product (often by means of unequal exchange), while industrial capital expropriates it through the buying and selling of labour power. Here one would have to make some perhaps rather simplistic assumptions about the nature of capitalist development - the drive to accumulate, to extract a sur-plus, to free labour, to increase productivity, etc.

At the same time, the notion that capital has a free hand in such transformation is dubious. In other words, I would very much question the analytical usefulness of the approach which assumes that everything is as it is because it serves some purpose (function) to capital. Rather the critical concept of contradiction and constraints should be kept at the forefront of the analysis.

Firstly then, we should ask why the local system is no longer able to reproduce its own conditions of production and reproduction. This question can be phrased another way - how has it been integrated into the wider economy? Has the intervention of capital resulted in the commoditisation of labour and the means of production but not the product of labour, or has the product been commoditised but not the labour that produces it? Or have both been commoditised? Have new forms of production been introduced and with them new ways of organising production? Have new labour processes, or partial processes, been introduced? Have these new forms of organisation of production or the new labour processes led to contradictory effects at the level of access to means of production, access to employment, rates of fertility, and so on?

To illustrate these somewhat programmatic remarks, I will again refer to my own field work.

In the late nineteenth century, domestic manufacture of cloth declined rapidly in part because raw cotton supplies dwindled - the cotton producers were directing their product to England because of the American Civil War. At the same time there was an expansion of cotton production which drew men out of the area into temporary wage labouring; but women apparently were not utilised as held labour. One could note a number of clear disbalances developing between men and women under these circumstances: men's greater familiarity with the wider society including command of Spanish; their ability to shed responsibilities for child-care through absence and the conversion of this responsibility into the gender-specific responsibility of the wife, recognised through handing over some part of the wage; and the reversal of economic roles - from the man now came the essential inputs into other labour processes (including that of the wife who could now only weave if she had manufactured yarn). This out-migration flow ceased quite rapidly after coffee growing was introduced forcibly into the area. Each household was obliged to grow a certain number of coffee bushes by the local political boss (or cacique) who combined with the coffee merchants to "encourage" production and yet keep coffee prices low. Land, as will be remembered, had always effectively been controlled by men, both at the household and the community level, even though inheritance was bilateral. With the perennial cash crop (coffee bushes, once planted, continue to produce for some 30 years or more) there was a double pressure to expand land use: both for coffee bushes and for the traditional subsistence crops, for coffee growing was grafted onto the traditional food cropping and did not replace it. This led to individualisation of land holding as well as to the gradual exclusion of women from land ownership. In turn there was a process of dispossession: this affected those families who already had claims to very small amounts of land as well as those who were not politically strong or adept enough to maintain what rights they had.

Coffee growing also implied a changed organisation of production: large- or small-scale reciprocal labour exchanges rapidly diminished, and production both of coffee and of the subsistence

crops (but not so markedly) was carried out on the basis of household labour resources. This individuated mode of working was
accentuated by competition between households for land and privileged access to the merchant and/or cacique. The social conditions were thereby laid for an emphasis on the importance of
familial labour, in other words, for large families. At the
individual level, larger numbers of sons and daughters ensured
sufficient supplies of unpaid familial labour for subsistence and
coffee production, but at the community level, since land supplies
were restricted, it meant ever increasing pressure on land and
ever larger numbers of families without access to land, or access
only to portions of land so small that they could not produce enough
for necessary consumption. There was in effect a surplus of labour
in the area and at this point (around the turn of the century) no
alternative jobs.

The effect on women was varied. They did not become more
involved in subsistence labouring than before; rather, they
became deskilled. They fell from the status of income-generating
skilled weavers to unpaid familial labourers controlling none of
the proceeds of their labour nor in charge of the totality of the
labour process. The nature of the labour process was also such
that the women's annual cycle of labour expenditure greatly
worsened: by this I mean that as weavers, women could fit their
activities into the general routine of housekeeping, food preparation, child-bearing and caring throughout the whole year. There
were only a few seasonal peaks requiring extra expenditure of
energy: the most important being the maize harvest which came at a
time of relatively abundant food supplies (maize is harvested dry).
With the change in the nature of production and the organisation of
production, as well as the change in the means of access to labour,
the women's annual cycle was greatly altered. Two seasonal peaks
now had to be accommodated as well as most probably an increase in
time and energy spent in pregnancy and lactation.

In this brief excursion into an empirical example, the contradictions brought both to the productive system itself and to women,
in particular, are quite clear. The introduction of coffee sets in
train both a reorganisation of production, of the relations of production and a different pattern of use of land. This in turn
encourages individuation and differentiation and the "freeing" of
certain categories of people from ownership of the land at the same
time that a higher rate of population growth is encouraged. The
two forms of production (embodied in a number of concrete labour
processes) are insufficient to reproduce the material conditions for
the maintenance of the population. In part, this is a consequence
of the nature of the way in which integration into the wider economy
has been achieved - through the intervention of mercantile capital
which has commoditised the product of a set of labour processes but
not labour itself. Women's participation in the total labour process of producing coffee is minimal: they are not in effective
possession of the plots of land, nor do they co-ordinate the total
labour process; rather, they intervene at only one part of the
production process (albeit a critical one, that of harvesting the
coffee berries). Lastly, they are not in control of the product
of their labour. Through the loss of control of their own
speciality their subordinate position vis-à-vis their men is
accentuated, and with growing individuation of households, the
potential for their social isolation is increased. At the same
time, the reorganisation of production and the need for supplies of
unremunerated labour lays stress on their child-bearing capacities:

women become more and more centred upon child-bearing and rearing, and pronatalist elements in the culture become stressed. High rates of child mortality necessitate high rates of fertility, while privatisation of land accentuates the importance of legitimate paternity. Women's importance as economic agents becomes subordinated to their importance as bearers of children. But pronatalism for the community as a whole spells disaster.

In such a meeting as this one at the ILO, one should perhaps try to outline why one's approach is at all useful for those who are trying to devise policies which will at best forward the aspirations of women, or at least ameliorate their living conditions.

It seems to me that only when one has a clear understanding of the processes of social change, and in particular an understanding of the working of the capitalist system, even if it is at quite a high level of abstraction, is it possible to begin to see how this will affect rural production systems in a number of distinct ways. This in turn should give one a basis upon which to suggest interventions which will not merely alleviate women's burdens but potentially lead to a more fundamental restructuring of the particular sets of social relations in which women are enmeshed often to the detriment of their own personal development.

I have tried to show in this brief note how the assumption that development inevitably pushes women into the subsistence sector is not adequate for a total understanding of the process. I would like to argue that women's new role as unremunerated familial labour on systems of small-scale production for the market is as prejudicial to their interests as their marginalisation in the subsistence sector.

B. SEX ROLES AND THE DIVISION OF
    LABOUR IN RURAL ECONOMIES

Some questions about the origin of the division
of labour by sex in rural societies: a summary

Lourdes Benería

I. Introduction

Available estimates of the world's working population grossly
underestimate women's participation in economic activities and cannot
tell us much about what types of tasks women perform in terms of the
existing gender-related division of labour. Yet we have reached a
period in history in which the most basic tenets and assumptions
influencing roles and power relationships between men and women in
society have been called into question, and these include the existing division of labour by sex. This calls for an analysis of the
factors determining this division - with the objective of pointing
towards directions of change that will lead to the elimination of
inequalities between the sexes.

I propose that it is useful to elaborate on the thesis that the
focal point of women's economic activities is given by their special
role in the reproduction of the labour force. It can be argued that
this role is at the root of the different forms that patriarchy takes
in different societies. Women's participation in production, the
nature of their work and the division of labour between the sexes
can then be viewed as a result of women's reproductive functions,
and conditioned by the nature of the productive process and by the
requirements of a given pattern of growth and accumulation.

II. Patriarchy and reproduction

The essence of male domination and the different patriarchal
forms through which male domination manifests itself have developed
around the need to control reproduction in its different aspects.
Reproduction implies the transmission of control of resources from
one generation to the next. In class society this process requires
that the subjects to whom control is passed on be identified. It
is to Engels' credit to have pointed out that the subordinate position of women can be attributed to the historical transformation
from communal to class societies linked to the institutionalisation
of private property. Private property generated the need to
identify its heirs. While maternity is always identifiable by the
community, paternity may be difficult to trace unless a clear-cut
control over women's sexuality is introduced. Hence the strict
control developed by most societies over women's reproductive activities. Despite the criticisms developed around Engels' thesis,
it is argued that to the extent that reproduction implies the
individual transmission of access to resources - be it private
property or not - the need to identify the beneficiaries of that
transmission remains.

The control over women's reproductive activities therefore
becomes the essence of male domination and the focal point for the
analysis of women's subordination. It is in this light that

institutions such as female seclusion and the segregation of the sexes, the harsh punishment of women's adultery, female circumcision and the restriction of women's mobility, need to be seen. It is also in this light that factors such as the role of ideology and religion in controlling women's sexuality and in rationalising their subordination must be understood.

Control over reproduction takes place at two levels, the private and the public. The first has its roots at the family level and corresponds to the range of customs, traditions and other expressions of civil society. The public level refers to the apparatus of state institutions dealing with order and political power. The inter-action between the two levels tends to increase in modern society and the split between the two can result in contradictions with regard to matters concerning reproduction. Thus, while most major world religions have tended to be "pronatalist" - a reflection of their being rooted in the rural world - a great number of governments have adopted a positive attitude towards family planning and population control. It is in the context of these contradictions that changes in fertility rates and population policies, with their effects on women, must be understood.

Two basic consequences derive from the control exercised over women's reproductive activities. One is that the focal point of their work becomes the household since it is in the household that activities related to physical reproduction are concentrated. This is the basis of the traditional division of labour by which domestic activities are seen exclusively as women's domain. The second consequence is the restriction of women's mobility which is prevalent in most societies, although in different degrees of intensity.

III. Production and the sexual division of labour

A. Domestic work

The extent to which domestic work is considered to be women's work in all societies is overwhelming and the reason must be sought in their reproductive functions. The inter-relationship between reproductive and productive activities at the domestic level makes it very difficult to draw a clear-cut distinction between the two when analysing in detail the breakdown of women's activities and the gender-related division of labour. This is especially so if we view production as part of the over-all process of reproduction, as argued by Meillassoux. In subsistence economies, domestic work contains a high degree of production geared to the household's own consumption - in contrast to the case of an urban family in which consumption becomes increasingly more dependent on goods produced outside of the household.

This implies that domestic activities must be viewed as playing two integrated functions centred around: (a) physical reproduction and other aspects of the reproduction of the labour force, and (b) production of use values. The content and nature of these functions depend upon factors that transcend the household - which in turn implies that women's domestic activities must be analysed within the context of the dynamics of an economic system in the process of transformation.

Sex roles and the division of labour:
rural women in Poland

Barbara Tryfan

While discussing the changes that have taken place in the life of rural women in Poland, it is necessary to emphasise the ambivalence that exists between their social position, on the one hand, and the functions that they perform, on the other. Despite the progressive improvement in their condition, the pattern of their daily existence still differs from the postulated model. The gap between the role assigned to them and their actual function, as well as the disproportion between village and town, results from differences in economic and social conditions, as well as from differences in family models. Rural families are influenced by traditional patterns of living and by attitudes that have been developing for centuries. At the same time, these families are influenced by urban living, an influence which modifies attitudes and views. In this clash of cultures and systems, rural women constantly face the difficult problem of choosing between the requirements of production and their own good.

Several factors have favourably affected the condition of rural women. One of them has to do with the new contractual forms of marriage. The traditional contract often used to be a humiliating and unfair transaction for the women. As a result of the economic changes that have taken place, a liberation from the influence of property factors has improved the conditions under which women enter into the marriage contract.

Child-bearing was another factor which used to determine unfavourably the situation of rural women. In the past, maternity was a tremendous burden due to a large average family size. In Poland, the birth rate has been declining since the late fifties. The decline has been registered in both rural and urban areas, although in urban areas it was observed earlier and the rate of decrease has been much faster.

The third positive change has been an improvement in the relative social position of rural women. This did not result from a sudden change of views but from changes in the economic position of women. Growing male employment outside of the farms generated the need for women to actually take over the main responsibilities of the farm. Thus, the range of activities and of decisions made by women has changed. Women now engage in trade, hire machines and negotiate loans for investment in other projects.

Consequently, a differentiation between men's and women's decisions is taking place. The use of family resources is also changing. Two "financial models" of a rural family can be distinguished. When agriculture provides the only source of income, the cash obtained from agricultural outputs is used in common in most cases. When other sources of income are available, the money obtained from farming is usually under the wife's control. This is again a sign of the widening responsibilities of rural women.

A fourth factor affecting the living conditions of rural women is the change in the division of work in the family. In the past, the division of labour was linked to a lower appreciation of activities performed by women. Gradually the strict barriers between

B.   Non-domestic production

Despite the fact that what is considered to be women's or men's work outside of the household varies from country to country, some generalisations can be made from emerging patterns of women's work. Women's economic tasks tend to concentrate on five types of activities which can be summarised as follows:

First, activities compatible with women's reproductive functions - which imply a low degree of physical mobility, not only because of the control exercised over women's sexuality, but also because the care of children automatically reduces mobility. Women, for example, tend to perform tasks close to the household, such as the processing of food and taking care of domestic animals, and nomadic women concentrate on camp-based activities more than nomadic men do.

Second, rural women's activities differ according to rural class hierarchies. Despite the fact that patriarchal institutions affect women of all classes, important differences exist between the work performed by women according to their household's access to productive resources. In households where outside agricultural workers are hired, for example, women tend to concentrate on domestic activities rather than agricultural work.

Third, activities subordinated to men's work are also subject to age hierarchies. The subordination of women's activities to men's can be observed even in cases where, as in many African societies, the economic independence of women is relatively high. On the other hand, an age-related division of labour can be observed in rural communities. This is so for household as well as non-domestic tasks.

Fourth, women's productive activities are often an extension of their household work. This is the case with tasks which are typically considered female rather than male work. Handweaving and handicrafts are typical and very common examples. It is interesting to point out that some of these activities, such as carrying water, require a great deal of physical strength.

Finally, when women work as wage earners, they are concentrated in the least permanent and the least paid activities. Their primary concentration in tasks related to reproduction has two main consequences. One is that for patriarchal society, production is men's primary concentration; women's involvement in the area of production is viewed as secondary to their pre-productive activities - hence the basis for their marginality and secondary role in production. In addition, women's earnings are viewed as complementary and not as a primary source of family income - hence the basis for women's low earnings and for wage discrimination.

IV.   The sexual division of labour:
a dynamic perspective

In the previous section, the analysis of the types of activities women perform is presented in a static form. Yet women's work at all levels can best be understood when it is placed within the perspective of an economic system in the process of transformation. In this sense, it can be argued that women's roles need to be analysed within the context of several key factors which include changes related to: (a) agrarian structures and modes of production; (b) availability of labour resources and development of labour markets; (c) the process of economic growth and accumulation; and (d) linkages between the local economy and the national and international markets.

First, the relationship between agrarian structures and women's roles in rural economies was already pointed out by Boserup. Women's participation in agriculture varies according to land tenure systems and the mode of production generated by patterns of land ownership. This implies that changes in the mode of production need to be analysed from the perspective of how they affect the sexes in a different way, a dimension that has often been neglected.

Second, another factor to take into consideration is the availability of labour resources. Thus, labour redundancy tends to displace women from employment in greater numbers than men - as in India today - and a pattern of predominantly male migration from the rural areas tends to increase women's workload at the same time that women take over activities previously performed by men.

Third, women's work is influenced by the dynamic forces behind a process of growth and accumulation. For example, the penetration of the market into subsistence agriculture and the introduction of commercial crops have often eroded the productive functions that women held in subsistence economies. In the same way, the strengthening of private property under colonial regimes and the disappearance of communal land tenure rights have tended to dispossess women of land and decrease their control over productive resources by recognising men as the new owners of land.

Finally, women's work must be placed within the context of the linkages between their activities and the national and international markets. It is in this sense that women's place in the accumulation process takes its full perspective and it is also in this sense that the analysis of the division of labour included in the previous section can best be understood. Numerous examples of commercialisation of crops provide illustrations of how the penetration of the market economy into traditional farming has affected women's work differently from men's.

There is, therefore, a dimension in the process of growth and accumulation, and in the development of national and international markets which has to do with how it can affect women differently from men. This dimension must be analysed in addition to the effects that this process has on both sexes and on different classes.

Two implications of this analysis can be pointed out. One is that an understanding of the dynamic forces that affect the structure of production is necessary in order to acquire an historical perspective of the changes in the division of labour by sex and of how it affects the position of women in society. The other is that sex roles are subject to change and need not be viewed as "natural" or "given". Viewed from this perspective, the traditional division of labour related to reproductive activities also becomes subject to change.

V. Concluding comments

What this implies is that all types of policies and changes regarding the position of women in social production and in society are subject to the limits imposed upon them by their reproductive role. It also points towards the fundamental importance of reproduction in determining the division of labour between men and women inside and outside the household; population policies, fertility rates, infant mortality rates, school attendance, and the availability of services such as nurseries and medical facilities become important variables that bear upon the restrictions placed upon women by their role in reproduction. Finally, this analysis implies that policies and programmes aiming at eliminating the subordination of women are bound to be incomplete unless they also focus on the household level, that is, on the role of men and women within the domestic economy.[1]

---

[1] A more detailed elaboration of these points can be found in my paper "Production Reproduction and the Sexual Division of Labour", ILO Working Paper, WEP 10/WP2, 1978.

B. Non-domestic production

Despite the fact that what is considered to be women's or men's work outside of the household varies from country to country, some generalisations can be made from emerging patterns of women's work. Women's economic tasks tend to concentrate on five types of activities which can be summarised as follows:

First, activities compatible with women's reproductive functions - which imply a low degree of physical mobility, not only because of the control exercised over women's sexuality, but also because the care of children automatically reduces mobility. Women, for example, tend to perform tasks close to the household, such as the processing of food and taking care of domestic animals, and nomadic women concentrate on camp-based activities more than nomadic men do.

Second, rural women's activities differ according to rural class hierarchies. Despite the fact that patriarchal institutions affect women of all classes, important differences exist between the work performed by women according to their household's access to productive resources. In households where outside agricultural workers are hired, for example, women tend to concentrate on domestic activities rather than agricultural work.

Third, activities subordinated to men's work are also subject to age hierarchies. The subordination of women's activities to men's can be observed even in cases where, as in many African societies, the economic independence of women is relatively high. On the other hand, an age-related division of labour can be observed in rural communities. This is so for household as well as non-domestic tasks.

Fourth, women's productive activities are often an extension of their household work. This is the case with tasks which are typically considered female rather than male work. Handweaving and handicrafts are typical and very common examples. It is interesting to point out that some of these activities, such as carrying water, require a great deal of physical strength.

Finally, when women work as wage earners, they are concentrated in the least permanent and the least paid activities. Their primary concentration in tasks related to reproduction has two main consequences. One is that for patriarchal society, production is men's primary concentration; women's involvement in the area of production is viewed as secondary to their pre-productive activities - hence the basis for their marginality and secondary role in production. In addition, women's earnings are viewed as complementary and not as a primary source of family income - hence the basis for women's low earnings and for wage discrimination.

IV. The sexual division of labour:
     a dynamic perspective

In the previous section, the analysis of the types of activities women perform is presented in a static form. Yet women's work at all levels can best be understood when it is placed within the perspective of an economic system in the process of transformation. In this sense, it can be argued that women's roles need to be analysed within the context of several key factors which include

changes related to: (a) agrarian structures and modes of production; (b) availability of labour resources and development of
labour markets; (c) the process of economic growth and accumulation;
and (d) linkages between the local economy and the national and
international markets.

First, the relationship between agrarian structures and women's
roles in rural economies was already pointed out by Boserup.
Women's participation in agriculture varies according to land tenure
systems and the mode of production generated by patterns of land
ownership. This implies that changes in the mode of production
need to be analysed from the perspective of how they affect the
sexes in a different way, a dimension that has often been neglected.

Second, another factor to take into consideration is the
availability of labour resources. Thus, labour redundancy tends
to displace women from employment in greater numbers than men -
as in India today - and a pattern of predominantly male migration
from the rural areas tends to increase women's workload at the same
time that women take over activities previously performed by men.

Third, women's work is influenced by the dynamic forces behind
a process of growth and accumulation. For example, the penetration
of the market into subsistence agriculture and the introduction of
commercial crops have often eroded the productive functions that
women held in subsistence economies. In the same way, the
strengthening of private property under colonial regimes and the
disappearance of communal land tenure rights have tended to dispossess
women of land and decrease their control over productive resources
by recognising men as the new owners of land.

Finally, women's work must be placed within the context of the
linkages between their activities and the national and international
markets. It is in this sense that women's place in the accumulation
process takes its full perspective and it is also in this sense that
the analysis of the division of labour included in the previous
section can best be understood. Numerous examples of commercialisation of crops provide illustrations of how the penetration of the
market economy into traditional farming has affected women's work
differently from men's.

There is, therefore, a dimension in the process of growth and
accumulation, and in the development of national and international
markets which has to do with how it can affect women differently
from men. This dimension must be analysed in addition to the
effects that this process has on both sexes and on different classes.

Two implications of this analysis can be pointed out. One
is that an understanding of the dynamic forces that affect the
structure of production is necessary in order to acquire an historical perspective of the changes in the division of labour by sex and
of how it affects the position of women in society. The other is
that sex roles are subject to change and need not be viewed as
"natural" or "given". Viewed from this perspective, the traditional
division of labour related to reproductive activities also becomes
subject to change.

V. Concluding comments

What this implies is that all types of policies and changes regarding the position of women in social production and in society are subject to the limits imposed upon them by their reproductive role.   It also points towards the fundamental importance of reproduction in determining the division of labour between men and women inside and outside the household; population policies, fertility rates, infant mortality rates, school attendance, and the availability of services such as nurseries and medical facilities become important variables that bear upon the restrictions placed upon women by their role in reproduction.   Finally, this analysis implies that policies and programmes aiming at eliminating the subordination of women are bound to be incomplete unless they also focus on the household level, that is, on the role of men and women within the domestic economy.[1]

---

[1] A more detailed elaboration of these points can be found in my paper "Production Reproduction and the Sexual Division of Labour", ILO Working Paper, WEP 10/WP2, 1978.

Sex roles and the division of labour:
rural women in Poland

Barbara Tryfan

While discussing the changes that have taken place in the life of rural women in Poland, it is necessary to emphasise the ambivalence that exists between their social position, on the one hand, and the functions that they perform, on the other. Despite the progressive improvement in their condition, the pattern of their daily existence still differs from the postulated model. The gap between the role assigned to them and their actual function, as well as the disproportion between village and town, results from differences in economic and social conditions, as well as from differences in family models. Rural families are influenced by traditional patterns of living and by attitudes that have been developing for centuries. At the same time, these families are influenced by urban living, an influence which modifies attitudes and views. In this clash of cultures and systems, rural women constantly face the difficult problem of choosing between the requirements of production and their own good.

Several factors have favourably affected the condition of rural women. One of them has to do with the new contractual forms of marriage. The traditional contract often used to be a humiliating and unfair transaction for the women. As a result of the economic changes that have taken place, a liberation from the influence of property factors has improved the conditions under which women enter into the marriage contract.

Child-bearing was another factor which used to determine unfavourably the situation of rural women. In the past, maternity was a tremendous burden due to a large average family size. In Poland, the birth rate has been declining since the late fifties. The decline has been registered in both rural and urban areas, although in urban areas it was observed earlier and the rate of decrease has been much faster.

The third positive change has been an improvement in the relative social position of rural women. This did not result from a sudden change of views but from changes in the economic position of women. Growing male employment outside of the farms generated the need for women to actually take over the main responsibilities of the farm. Thus, the range of activities and of decisions made by women has changed. Women now engage in trade, hire machines and negotiate loans for investment in other projects.

Consequently, a differentiation between men's and women's decisions is taking place. The use of family resources is also changing. Two "financial models" of a rural family can be distinguished. When agriculture provides the only source of income, the cash obtained from agricultural outputs is used in common in most cases. When other sources of income are available, the money obtained from farming is usually under the wife's control. This is again a sign of the widening responsibilities of rural women.

A fourth factor affecting the living conditions of rural women is the change in the division of work in the family. In the past, the division of labour was linked to a lower appreciation of activities performed by women. Gradually the strict barriers between

the duties traditionally performed by husband and wife are being
eliminated and the division of duties adapted to the actual needs
of the new situation.   As a result, women often perform tasks which
used to be considered men's tasks, such as harvest work.   At the
same time, men become involved in activities that were traditionally
performed by women.   For example, cow milking and cattle feeding
are very often done by men now.   Thus, women are performing new
tasks outside of the home, while men's activities are moving closer
to the household.

Despite these favourable changes, rural women's living and
working conditions are difficult.   It can often be observed that,
parallel to their rise in social status, an increase in the burden
of their responsibilities has also taken place.   The first reason
for this is that women play a major role in farming and the care
of animals.   In spite of the progress made in land mechanisation
and all kinds of services, the average working time of rural women
has not decreased during the last 40 years;   on the contrary, the
trend is an expansionary one.

In more general terms, the overburden of contemporary rural
women results from their new role in agricultural production - a
consequence of men's participation in outside employment and from
growing family requirements.   Women, wives of peasant workers, are
in charge of farm services, the selling of agricultural products,
daily domestic chores and children's care.   In fact, women have
become heads of families and production managers and, to a higher
degree than ever before, they are full-time workers at various
levels.

In view of the growing requirements of a contemporary rural
family, labour-saving household appliances may limit the working
time of the housewife, but at the same time they widen the sphere
of her activities.   Thus, it is not a reduction in working time
which occurs, but a relief from hard physical work.   All these
additional burdens are viewed as "the price" of modern life.
However, this price does not seem to be equally distributed among
all family members in proportion to their strength and possibilities;
it falls heavily on women who undoubtedly bear the greatest responsibility for their own promotion and that of their family.

The scope of women's work in the household and in agriculture
is also influenced by the development of a new attitude towards
children in rural families, connected with a new concept of social
responsibility towards them.   Rural women, indeed, give birth to
fewer children than in the past, but the care for the children is
much greater.

In view of the specific character of rural family life,
problems of social policy, in particular social and legal protective
measures for maternity and family, become especially important.
Besides the promotion of mechanisation and of vital services, the
issues of social assistance to families are an important element in
the improvement of living conditions of rural women.

C.   EFFECTS OF THE PENETRATION OF
      THE MARKET ON RURAL WOMEN'S WORK

Women in subsistence production in Ghana

Jette Bukh

This abstract refers to a study which analyses the historical
process of integration and subordination of a rural area into the
market economy in the southern part of the Volta region in Ghana.
The dynamics of the expansion of early colonial commodity exchange
introduced commodity production into the local economy, which in
the 1920s and 1930s became an export economy based on cocoa.   The
colonial economy generated new social differentiations and a pattern
of migration that made the area play a dual role: as a cash-crop
producer, and as a source of labour supply.   Within this period
both the over-all social organisation and the relations of production changed.   The land became more privatised in the sense that
although the lineage community kept ownership, the control of the
land was lost with the redistribution that took place between its
users, that is, between households.   In addition, the organisation
of production changed, particularly with the increased importance
of cash income and wage labour, resulting in traditional labour
services within the lineage community being substituted with wage
labour.   The new economic pattern brought increasing economic
differentiation between households within the same lineage.

Dissolution of lineage solidarity and the progressive impact of
migration resulted in a general break-up of traditional structures,
including marriage practices and the patterns of control over
children.   Many of the functions of the old family and lineage
organisation were taken over by households, which became much more
isolated as production and consumption units.

With the introduction of cacao and the increasing importance of
predominantly male migration, there was a general change in the
sexual division of labour; women took over more responsibilities for
food crop production.   But the changes took place not only at a
general level; they penetrated the household structure and the
division of labour within the household.   This transformation
brought women into a much more central position vis-à-vis the
survival of many rural families.   Almost half the households are
now headed by women, and most of these households have no male
members.   About two-thirds of the rural women are solely responsible
for the daily upkeep of themselves and their children.   Household
consumption levels have not only been affected by this situation,
caused primarily by male migration; in addition, marriage practices
have changed.

The age of marriage has increased for both women and men, and
divorces are common, resulting in many adults living without a spouse.
Children are left more to women now than traditionally, while their
productive capacity has been gradually restricted due to increasing
school attendance.   Although they help women in domestic tasks, they
are not the economic input that traditionally made a man with many
children a wealthy man.   They now represent a cost and do not give
much security for old age.

The division of labour by sex within households has also been distorted by the introduction of cash earnings, as access to cash income has become unevenly distributed between men and women. Men control the most important sources of cash earnings - cocoa production and wage labour - while women's earnings have been determined by whatever small surplus the day-to-day subsistence activities could yield. Men and women also use their cash differently. While men, and particularly younger men, often use their cash to buy goods for themselves - "bachelors' consumption goods" - the women's little money is usually used to cover certain household expenses.

The disintegration of traditional lineage and family structures, has left a major part of rural subsistence responsibilities in the hands of women. The consequence of this development for the livelihood of rural households can only be fully understood when certain difficulties facing women due to the existence of traditional patriarchal structures are taken into consideration. These structures operate mainly at a practical level through differences in access to essential resources such as land, labour, cash, education and know-how, in relation to which men are privileged.

In relation to land, women have only secondary rights and only through males. With the increasing privatisation of land, combined with a tendency to preserve land resources because of an apparent decrease in soil fertility in the area, women's access to land has also become more difficult. They now have to rely on individual men's willingness to let them use their personal fallow land, instead of being allocated a piece of the common lineage land, as was done traditionally. At the same time, the availability of labour is a factor women must consider in their choice of land, because time is women's scarcest resource, they prefer land that does not need too much work to clear. Otherwise they need to hire labour to do the clearing.

Women only dispose of their own and part of the children's labour. As mentioned earlier, children do not participate in much productive work, although older girls, those between 12-14 years of age, do help in domestic tasks. For example, they spend about a quarter of the time adult women devote to cooking, although they rarely take full responsibility by themselves. While men dispose of some female labour, the only way that women can get access to extra adult labour, is by employing wage labourers. Women's own labour time is cut into short intervals because of domestic tasks, particularly the care of children. Women's labour problem determines the kind of economic activities in which they can engage; they tend to concentrate on activities which allow them to perform different tasks at the same time.

The kind of economic activities in which women can engage are also determined by the amount of cash that they have available for investment. Women have few possibilities of getting access to capital, especially to relatively large amounts. The responsibility for the daily needs of the household also prevents them from accumulating cash earnings. As a result, women's economic activities are continuously kept at a very small scale, with little profit.

The context in which the patriarchal structures most openly operate at an ideological level is in relation to women's access to school education. Differences in expectations of boys and girls in regard to schooling, make girls start dropping out of school around the age of 12-13.   The ideology works at two levels.   Since girls are expected to stay home and look after the house and, later on, children, education for them is considered to be a waste.   In addition, girls are expected to do housework from an early age, and indeed do so, while boys are not.   Their motivation to stay at school is therefore greatly reduced.

The way in which women manage to fulfil their role as providers of subsistence, is by combining a lot of different productive activities like farming, petty trading, processing of agricultural crops, etc.   All their activities are performed on a small scale and within the flexible frame of the informal sector.   The double pressure on women, as providers of subsistence and facing diffi- culties in gaining access to strategic resources, limits their choice of land and crops.   Women have to choose the easy, accessible land, which is the less fertile land, and crops that demand little labour input.   This is why they have switched from yams to production of the less nutritious cassava.   Women's agricultural output therefore suffers from both low productivity and low nutritional value.

Women do not react passively to this increased subordination, but their means of defence are few and limited in scope.   Therefore, their reactions are mostly on an individual basis, as personal protests, although there are signs that women are trying to organise themselves to solve some of their daily problems.

The study of rural women and the development of capitalism in Colombian agriculture

Magdalena León de Leal and
Carmen Diana Deere

This study analyses the changes that have been introduced in the sexual division of labour by the development of capitalism in Colombian agriculture.   We start from the premise that the study of women cannot be undertaken in isolation from the study of society, nor of the process of social change.   The process of change encompassed by the development of capitalist social relations in the rural areas provides the analytical framework through which to view the changes in the form of incorporation of the peasantry into the wider economy, its impact on the peasant household labour process, and consequently, on the division of labour by sex.

Our historical analysis builds on the inter-relationship between international, national, regional and local processes of change.   We first take into account the changing mode of incorporation of the Colombian social formation as a peripheral, dependent social structure into the world capitalist system.   The changing requirements of the world market have, in turn, influenced the pattern of integration of different regions into the national social formation during different historical periods.   At the regional level, differing forms of integration into the national economy, for example, as a supplier of wage goods or of export commodities, have been characterised by the development of economic and social institutions which correspond to distinct social relations of production.   Identification of the relations of production which peasants enter into enables us to analyse the inter-relationship between the peasant household and the mechanisms of surplus extraction in rural areas, in terms of its implications for the division of labour by sex and for peasant women's socio-economic position.

Our analysis focuses on four rural areas of Colombia, each characterised by one of the following processes of integration into the national economy: one region (Fredonia) became integrated as a commodity producer (of coffee) for the world market during the late nineteenth century; two regions (Espinal and Sincelejo) became integrated as commercial agricultural producers for the national market during the twentieth century; and finally, one region (García Rovira) has been a source of migrant labour for other areas throughout the twentieth century.[1]   Each form of integration corresponds to a particular agrarian structure and to a unique process of internal change in the relations of production, with important repercussions for the peasant economy.

The regions of El Espinal and Sincelejo are characterised by the development of agrarian capitalist enterprises from what once were haciendas, in response to the development of the Colombian internal market in the twentieth century.   In these areas, the

---

[1] The data presented here is based on four months of field work in each region carried out by ACEP (Colombian Association of Population Studies) researchers in the second stage of a two-year research project.

stimulus of the internal market fostered the growth of a market in
land concomitant with the proletarianisation of the peasantry.
What stands out today in these regions is the strong integration of
the peasantry into the labour market, which forms a local labour
reserve to meet the seasonally fluctuating demands of agricultural
production on the commercial farms.

In contrast, capitalist development in the coffee region of
Fredonia was brought about with the integration of Colombia into
the world market. In this area, we see the development of a
labour market in the late nineteenth century in response to the
labour intensive requirements of coffee production on haciendas.
A sector of independent peasant producers also became integrated
into the international coffee market.

In the region of García Roviro the process of minifundisation
has been dominant. As the peasantry has lost access to sufficient
land to meet its subsistence requirements, it has become increasingly integrated into not just the regional, but also the national
and international labour markets. This region, while characterised
by an extreme ecological situation and poor infrastructure, none the
less produces an agricultural surplus which is captured by a local
petty bourgeoisie in the form of rent. This brief background
allows us to consider the changes that have been introduced in the
sexual division of labour concomitant to each process.

What immediately stands out in a historical analysis is that
under non-capitalist relations of production, the peasant family
has been the primary unit of production and the primary unit subject
to exploitation. First of all, peasant families were responsible
for opening up the virgin land of the regions of Sincelejo and
El Espinal in the nineteenth century. This amounted to a form of
indirect appropriation of surplus, since once the lands became
cultivable they were rapidly appropriated by the landed elite.
The value of the family's labour was reflected in the increasing
price of land.

Under the hacienda system, significant differences are evident
in the sexual division of labour, depending on the particular
regional form of incorporation, as well as on the labour requirements of particular crops. At the beginning of the twentieth
century, the regions of Sincelejo and El Espinal were characterised
by the monopoly control over land by local elites engaged in cattle
raising. Peasant families gained usufruct rights to land through
the payment of rent in labour services, in kind or through share-
cropping. A characteristic of both regions is that the labour
services fell upon men. None the less, the peasant family was
obliged to carry on agricultural production for its own subsistence
requirements as well as for the payment of rent in kind. This
suggests the proposition that the greater or lesser participation
of women in agricultural production was directly related to the
extent that men were required to perform labour services for the
landowner. In Sincelejo, it appears that women's participation
in subsistence agricultural production was minimal, although in
the production of tobacco, a labour intensive crop par excellence,
women and children were active participants.

When coffee was introduced in the region of Fredonia, the
labour intensive nature of this crop again required the active
participation of all family members. On the haciendas where the
landowner directed the cultivation of the crop, both men and women

worked the fields, although work teams were segregated by sex.
On the individual usufruct parcels on the haciendas, the family was
the basic unit of production, and the unit subject to the appropriation of surplus through the payment of rent in kind.

Although large haciendas do not appear to have played a major
role in the region of García Rovira, lack of access to land forced
many peasant families to enter into non-capitalist relations of
production with the larger landowners. Here it appears that labour
service obligations for the usufruct of land fell upon the whole
peasant family. None the less, there was a strict division of
labour by sex in the particular labour services required. Men were
assigned to the fields whereas women were obliged to perform domestic
services for the landowner as well as being charged with animal care.

The development of capitalist agricultural enterprises
significantly changed the labour process as well as the sexual
division of labour. The integration of the region of El Espinal
into the national market, characterised by the entrance of new
capital into the rural areas and the capitalisation of the old
haciendas, caused the expulsion of many peasants from their usufruct
plots on the haciendas. This created a labour reserve in the semi-
urbanised rural areas on the one hand, and a large sector of semi-
proletarianised minifundistas on the other. The mechanisation of
many agricultural tasks consequently reduced the demand for
permanent agricultural labourers. It was generally men that were
employed as the permanent wage workers on the commercial farms.

None the less, the seasonally fluctuating demand for temporary
agricultural workers provided a stimulus for the semi-proletariani-
sation of women. We should recall that under the hacienda system,
women had worked in agricultural production, but only on their own
plots. While women generally did not work outside their own homes,
the increased pressures of rural poverty - exemplified in the
peasantry's declining access to land - has required that women go
out into the labour force, albeit on a temporary and seasonal basis.
Women in El Espinal today comprise a significant number of the
cotton pickers at harvest time. In the tobacco zone of this
region, women are also important as temporary wage workers in the
collection and processing of tobacco, as well as being employed on
the manufacturing side. Recently, with the installation of textile
factories in the region, the demand for female workers has increased.

Sincelejo, the other region characterised by the development
of capitalist agricultural enterprises, contrasts markedly with
El Espinal in that women have been almost totally excluded from
agricultural wage work. Female participation in cotton harvesting
is minimal, compared to the prevalence of female labour in this
activity in the other region. The differences which have resulted
in the sexual division of labour may be due to the varying over-all
labour market conditions which have characterised the development of
capitalist enterprises in successive periods. Whereas the development of capitalist agricultural enterprises in El Espinal took place
in the 1950s, when labour was relatively scarce, the rise of cotton
enterprises in Sincelejo was a product of the late 1960s and 1970s,
when surplus labour with respect to employment opportunities was a
marked feature of rural life.

None the less, in Sincelejo, women have continued working in
tobacco processing, an activity that has traditionally been
identified with female participation. Here the destruction of

family tobacco enterprises by commercial capital and the entrance of industrial capital into tobacco processing has led to the proletarianisation of women. They perform the same tasks in the factory that once were carried out in the home.

The development of the labour market in the coffee region of Fredonia in the twentieth century has been marked by a sizeable drop in female participation in the labour force. On the hacienda, women had participated in all aspects of coffee production; now their participation tends to be confined to the most labour-intensive tasks, such as coffee selection and processing.

In García Rovira, male proletarianisation has been geared to temporary migration to other zones over the last decades. Interestingly, the few employment opportunities that have arisen locally have been aimed at women. Women are the principal workers in the tobacco processing establishments; and the small-scale manufacturing enterprises started up in recent times have sought to engage female workers.

These four regional studies, while representing different processes of capitalist development in rural areas, support the hypothesis that women are important constituents of the labour reserve for capital. Women played a reserve labour function on the haciendas, and continue doing so for agricultural enterprises as well as on peasant commercial farms that employ wage labourers. Female proletarianisation, from the point of view of the demand for labour, has been closely geared to those crops that are labour intensive. The use of female wage labourers is also closely related to the maintenance of low wages. In addition, we should point out that the demand for female agricultural labourers has also tended to parallel the scarcity of available male workers. When men have alternative employment opportunities at high pay, women are encouraged to join the labour force, at much lower pay, serving to maintain low wages for capitalist development.

A characteristic of female proletarianisation in agricultural enterprises is that women tend to be paid, not per day worked, but rather in terms of piece work. This form of payment has assured that exploitation is still based on the family unit, since women are encouraged to take as many children with them as possible to aid in the picking of the crop or in weeding, for example. Piece work payment increases the total labour time which is subject to appropriation and ensures that a whole family must work in order to earn a minimal wage.

Within agrarian industrial enterprises, women wage workers serve to keep wages low through the sex-typing of jobs. Men and women perform different tasks, and since female tasks (generally the most labour intensive) are judged to be less "productive", a dual salary structure can be maintained at women's expense.

From the point of view of the supply of labour, female proletarianisation has been closely related to the economic necessities of the majority of the peasantry. Women join the rural labour force, even though there might be cultural sanctions against doing so, since they need to contribute to the family's maintenance in whatever way they can. Women's participation in temporary agricultural work is also closely related to the lack of alternative employment opportunities. Young women do have an alternative, not in the rural areas, but in migrating to the cities to obtain work as domestic servants. This has contributed to the very high rate of female rural-urban migration in Colombia. But migration is rarely an alternative for the married rural woman with children. She stays in the rural areas, obtains what work she can in agricultural activities at low pay.

Women's work on the home agricultural plot is also closely related to the phenomenon of rural poverty. In the four regions studied it was noted that women's increased participation in agricultural production was related to decreasing farm size and rural poverty. As the family loses access to the means of production, men are proletarianised, either locally or by migrating to other zones in search of work; generally women will remain on the farm, tending the crops and the animals.

Finally, we should note that in the four regions, notwithstanding women's participation in the labour force, or in subsistence agricultural production, women are always charged with the myriad of duties required for the daily maintenance of the family labour force.

Women and rural development in Africa
Marie-Angélique Savané

I. Rural women

In pre-colonial Black Africa, the work done by men and women
used to be divided fairly equally. The men did the work of
defending or attacking villages, hunted and looked after the larger
animals, cleared the ground, and cut trees for use in building
houses, granaries and enclosures. They also did metal, leather
and basket work. The agricultural work of women consisted of
hoeing, planting, weeding and looking after the granaries. They
also did all the household work: cooking, fetching water, picking
and preparing vegetables, looking after the children, cleaning
the house, etc. They also specialised in pottery, weaving and
basketry.

The sexual division of labour was so clear-cut that men rarely
called on women for help, or vice versa. In Senegal, for example,
the old system of farming, in which land used to grow millet one
year was left fallow the next, allowed a spacing of agricultural
work over the year making female labour unnecessary. Unlike the
men's work, however, women's work was more continuous and
monotonous. It was the work needed for the survival of the family,
and it gave women real independence.

Anthropologists have shown that although systems of farming
vary, they show a certain uniformity in the sexual division of
labour.[1] This is a pattern which can be clearly explained in the
context of subsistence economies in which men and women perform
specific tasks which have grown up over generations. However,
colonisation, which introduced a barter economy,[2] brought the
following changes:

- the imposition of a money economy which obliged peasants to
  produce goods that traders would be willing to buy;

- the replacement of locally produced handicrafts by imported
  manufactured products brought in by import-export companies;

- forced labour and forced production of certain crops, causing
  massive migration to mines or plantations;

- political support by the colonisers for the social classes
  and strata which were allowed to take over land, or

- an alliance with religious orders who chose to levy tithes
  in the form of items that could subsequently be sold.

---

[1] See Achola O. Pala, "La Femme africaine dans le développement
rural: orientations et priorités", Cahier OLC No. 12 (Dec.
1976), Institute for Development Studies, University of Nairobi.

[2] See J. Suret Canale, l'Afrique noire - l'Ere coloniale,
Editions Sociales, Paris, Chapter 1.

All these factors have contributed to bringing the traditional units of production, that is, family units, more and more into the capitalist system.

Social structures are being reorganised to suit this new economy. By obliging the head of the family (the man) to pay taxes, the labour power of the whole family is pressed into service to raise cash crops for export. These can only be grown by taking land and labour away from subsistence agriculture. And in order to make the sale of labour profitable, a new sexual division of labour has developed. This is either because the head of the family can no longer cultivate both cash and subsistence crops (in plantation areas of Africa), or because women have to do agricultural labour (in crop zones), or because the creation of a migratory labour force (native reserve areas) has left women with all the male tasks. In Kenya, for example, a mission carried out by the International Labour Office in 1972 on Employment, Incomes and Equality showed that about 525,000 households were headed by women. The men had emigrated to the towns.

Thus "the presence of the Europeans has modified the division of tasks, usually to the detriment of women ... Cultivating new crops for export has replaced the warrior preoccupations of men. Women have merely seen their burdens increase."[1] This division of labour, then, is due neither to the "wicked Africans" who oppress women, nor to natural aptitudes. It is the result of colonial and neo-colonial policies designed to organise the productive capacities of the family-based economy for the purpose of making profit.[2]

II. Women and production

Rural women comprise 70-90 per cent of the female population of African countries. They do 60 per cent of the agricultural work and provide many of the services needed for feeding the family - 44 per cent according to the United Nations Economic Commission for Africa.[3] The degree of participation of women in agricultural work, however, varies with the kind of farming and basic natural resources. Because West Africa lacks mineral wealth, the colonial powers were obliged to turn to the large scale production of tropical goods for export, under terms which would be attractive to the investors of the Centre. On the other hand, in the native reserve areas of Africa, the extensive mineral wealth (gold, diamonds, copper) and the kinds of agricultural settlements established by the colonists demanded an abundant work force. African communities were driven from their land and confined in poor areas. Men became temporary or permanent migrants. This is the Africa of bantustans and apartheid.

---

[1] D. Paulme et al., Femmes d'Afrique noire, Mouton and Co., Paris, The Hague, 1960, pp. 15-16.

[2] C. Meillassoux, Femmes, greniers et capitaux, Ed. Maspéro, Paris, 1975, p. 166.

[3] Panafrican Centre for Research and Education for Women - CEA, Addis Ababa.

(a) Crop-producing Africa

In the agricultural economy of crop-growing areas, the division between work and leisure time is defined by the productive and dead seasons which succeed each other throughout the year. This is why the work in subsistence farming is shared by both men and women. Produce for export - peanuts and cotton - is almost exclusively cultivated by men, while women are involved in the collective work of growing millet in the headman's fields. They also participate in weeding, harvesting, threshing and sifting, and in transporting millet.

Each year, the headman allocates independent plots of land to the women. This is done in exchange for work in the collective field. Women use these plots to grow some export crops (peanuts and cotton), and millet and sorghum. This produce is stored and then processed for selling. This is the major source of income for women. During the dry seasons, women also work irrigated plots on which vegetables are grown to provide a more varied and balanced daily diet for the family. The surplus is bartered or sold at the market. Thus, the staple food, millet, is provided by the husband, who is morally responsible for feeding the family. But the women will have done her share of work on the husband's farm in producing it.[1]

However, in areas which are isolated from transport systems and less suitable for growing export crops, women have the entire responsibility for growing crops, as their husbands often leave to sell their labour elsewhere. The money they send home, however, does help to alleviate the women's burden. This is the case in regions where there is extensive migration, as for example, among the Soninkés in Senegal, who go to France, or the Mossis in Upper Volta, who go to the Ivory Coast.

(b) Plantation Africa

Here, the period of fallow is shorter, and the productive and non-productive seasons come fairly close together. There are also two clearly different kinds of farming, distinguished by the crops grown, the outlets for them, and especially by the sexual division of labour in production. Men work on commercial farms (cacao, coffee, cola nuts, palm oil, pineapples, etc.) and women on subsistence farming (plantain, bananas, swamp rice, manioc, maize, vegetables, etc.). They also gather vegetal matter (palm oil nuts, avocados, etc.), wild plants and fruit.

Each year the men divide up the land among their various wives, who then work it with help from the children. The husbands cut, slash and burn to clear the land for their wives. The women do the rest of the preparatory work. The main field is used to grow subsistence crops for feeding the family. The women sometimes

---

[1] See Etude sur les conditions de vie et de travail des femmes en milieu rural et proposition d'un programme d'intervention régional pour l'allègement du travail des femmes, Sept. 1976, SAED, BP 593 Ouagadougou, Upper Volta. See also Claudine Vidal, Actions et réactions des femmes dans une zone en développement au Sénégal, Mémoire EOHE, Paris 1976. See also G. Belloncie, "Problèmes posés par la promotion de la femme rurale en Afrique de l'Ouest", in Leçons de l'expérience nigérienne d'animation féminine, IRAM.

have additional allotments where they grow herbs, roots and legumes.
Thus women produce all the food for the family, but in addition
actively participate in the work on the plantations. Women pick
coffee berries, for example, and carry them to the village. The
introduction of cash crops here has meant that women have new
obligations in addition to those they already had performed
traditionally.[1] The men become wage labourers on the big plantations,
but they eat the food produced domestically by their wives and
children.

III. Women and animal raising

In different agricultural systems, women usually look after
small animals and poultry, feeding them cereal husks and household
scraps. Sometimes women actually own these animals and can thus
use them as gifts to be given during ceremonies, for instance, or
as sacrifices in rituals. They can also trade them at the market.
The women of nomadic peoples own the larger animals which come
with their dowry.[2] Their task essentially is to process the milk
and other dairy products from these animals, which they then sell
or exchange for millet or maize from sedentary farmers.

IV. Agricultural tools and techniques

The various agricultural jobs discussed here are carried out
in very trying conditions for women:

- their personal fields are often scattered and far away from
  the main plots or the villages. In addition, they are
  relatively small and, because they are not intensively
  prepared for planting like the main plots, they are often
  full of roots and stumps;

- all the work must be done by hand, with traditional instruments
  like the daba or little knives for rice, maize or root crops,
  and a kind of metal implement on the end of a long stick for
  cutting fruit from trees;

- farming techniques are closely connected with the weather,
  which determines the kind of work done in the rainy or dry
  seasons. An exact calendar exists, for instance, for rice
  and maize cycles.

That these techniques are still used is due to the resistance
of the smallholding peasants to capital-intensive agriculture and
their preference for traditional forms of family subsistence
agriculture. Although this leads to low productivity in family
farming, the traditional system still provides something to fall
back on when conditions in commercial production become too
difficult.

---

[1] See Nicon Schöpflin, Difficultés et espoir de l'animation
féminine en pays Dida, Ivory Coast, 1972.

[2] Etude complémentaire sur le rôle et la place de la femme
sénégalaise dans le développement, Conseil Economique et Social,
Dakar, Dec. 1975, pp. 42-46.

V. Other activities

The economic role of women goes beyond simply cultivating the fields and picking the fruit and vegetables. After harvest, women process the raw produce. Grain, for example, has to be crushed, dried and ground into flour. This work requires long hours of pounding, sifting, sieving and cooking. Some vegetables are dried or kept in storage bins. Fruits are also processed into kerite butter.

Another important activity is handicrafts. The types vary from one region to another, and include pottery, weaving, dyeing basketry and tanning. This activity is, however, not as remunerative as it used to be, because of heavy competition from Western manufactured goods. Brewing and selling beer (from millet and maize) is also a fairly widespread female activity in Black Africa.

Itinerant markets are good outlets for the bartering or sale of these processed goods. They take place in the villages to which merchants sometimes travel long distances. Women go there to trade on their own account, selling imported products such as kitchen utensils, soap, fuel and sugar. Bartering also takes place between nomadic and sedentary peoples.

Tradition has sometimes favoured the participation of women in commerce, especially where, according to custom, they are responsible for feeding their children. The most typical cases of this are found in Ghana and Nigeria. According to Ester Boserup, half of the women of the Yoruba tribe of Nigeria are primarily engaged in commerce while in Ghana women account for 80 per cent of village and town trading. Sometimes these women form very strong and influential trading organisations. An example of this is the "fish mammies" in Ghana. In certain regions, women sell the produce from their harvests directly to large private companies or to the State.

VI. Women and property

(a) The problem of land ownership

Land used to be held in common under the joint control of the headmen. It served as a symbol of social cohesion. This collective aspect of land ownership has changed gradually with the imposition of cash cropping. The colonial administration declared itself the owner of so-called "unclaimed" land and chattels and refused to grant its protection or guarantees to other than individual holdings. "Thus, through the imposition of a registration scheme", says one author, "land previously held by custom and over which simple use rights prevailed, became the object of property rights".[1]

The market economy has brought with it a new system of land inheritance: increasingly, land rights go to male heirs, while the daughters are almost entirely excluded. This is the beginning of rural individualism. Since women have never been involved in land distribution, they also have been excluded from the new legal

---

[1] Guy Kouassigan, L'Homme et la Terre, Orstom, 1966 (cited by J. Bistilliat in La place de la femme dans le développement, OECD, 1977).

approach to land ownership. They have neither legal access to
land nor sufficient money to acquire it since they have almost no
income. However, since women are held responsible for feeding
their families, it is necessary that they have land to till. So,
every year, men are obliged to grant their wives the right to
use certain plots. This right of use is not definitive, being
limited to the length of time the land is under cultivation.
Moreover, such rights are ruled out in any case by the practice
of leaving land fallow every other year.

Thus, each year, married women are dependent upon the goodwill
of their husbands and the availability of land in order to grow
food. The men allocate the poorest and most remote plots to them
and keep the best land for themselves for the growing of cash
crops. Drought or erosion,[1] population growth and the economic
situation are other factors which help to make women marginal.

(b) Material possessions and money

Generally speaking, possessions which are used in common are
considered the property of the man. This is the case even when
they are most often used by the woman. In addition, women who
are deprived of a role in commerical agriculture tend to spend
what little income they have on the family and thus are unable
to save much.[2] This lack of money rules out the possibility of
divorce since women would be unable to pay back their dowries.
Thus, for the many women who cannot inherit or own land, the only
way to survive is to marry. The family often counts on the dowry
to resolve a number of financial problems (e.g. paying for a
brother's dowry, increasing the family's assets). And the husband
is the only person who can provide a woman with shelter and land
so that she can feed herself and fulfil her obligations as a
mother.

VII. Women and the modernisation of agriculture

The structure of commercial agriculture, the kinds of seeds,
plants and fertilizers available, the way co-operatives, rural
enterprises, the commercial infrastructure and the market are
organised, are all for the benefit of export production. This has
created not only regional distortions but also sexual discrimination
in rural labour:

"The introduction of technological and scientific methods of
farming has often contributed to the marginalisation of
women. Development projects, agricultural assistance
schemes, training in modern farming techniques, and the
acquisition of machines and land, generally have been conceived
with men in mind."[3]

---

[1] "L'exemple du Sénégal", in René Dumont, Paysanneries au
abois, 1972.

[2] Les Carnets de l'enfance, UNICEF, Oct.-Dec. 1976.

[3] Report of the FAO to the Commission on the Status of Women,
25th Session, 1970.

Moreover, technical innovations often increase women's work. Ester Boserup states that "women do 55 per cent of the agricultural work in a traditional village, and 68 per cent of the work in a village where sophisticated farming techniques are used".[1]

It has even become apparent in some countries that the introduction of new crops, while increasing the participation of women in the labour force, often fails to improve their income. In the Bouaké region of the Ivory Coast, for example, only 10-35 per cent of the family income goes to women as against 50 per cent in the traditional villages.[2]

The household unit becomes a vehicle for selling in the market economy and this creates divisions between the head of the family and its other members (women, children, other dependants). The former is the only family member who has access to credit, co-operatives and technical information. He becomes the salesman for household production and is the one who receives the pay for the family's work. "The man acquires new administrative roles as the supervisor of the family's labour and banker of its income, while the wife or wives take on some of the characteristics of a rural proletariat."[3]

Thus, the modernisation of agricultural techniques creates differences in levels of productivity between men and women, thereby increasing the inequality which already existed. Women's work, both in the home and on the family plot, receives no cash reward and produces a low yield, since no capital is invested in it. As Ingrid Palmer has suggested, a parallel can be established between the new economic relationship among men and women in rural areas and the "North-South gap" that is between the industrialised nations and the Third World.

---

[1] Boserup, op. cit., p. 21.

[2] Participation féminine au développement rural dans la région de Bouaké, Planning Ministry, Abidjan, 1968, p. 83

[3] I. Palmer, "Rural women and the basic-needs approach to development", International Labour Review, Vol. 115, No. 1, Jan-Feb. 1977.

D.   WOMEN AND RURAL DEVELOPMENT

Women's participation in rural development: a Bangladesh pilot project

Tahrunnessa Abdullah

Women constitute 50 per cent of the human resources of Bangladesh and 90 per cent of them live in rural areas.   It is obvious that there cannot be any rural development programme without integration of rural women into the development process, not only as beneficiaries but as active participants.

I.   Women's programme under IRDP
     (Integrated Rural Development
     Programme)

IRDP has included women as an important and integral part of its comprehensive rural development programme; it has initiated projects in 25 "thanas" on an experimental basis.   The IRDP Pilot Project in Population Planning and Rural Women's Co-operatives came into being in 1974 with the purpose of exploring ways to integrate rural women in social and economic development.   The project is based on the assumption that given the chance, women and their families will respond to new economic opportunities and will participate in income-earning projects.   Once women are contributing regularly to the family income, they will begin to have more decision-making influence in such matters as family planning.   The goal of the project is the development of a model programme whereby village women can:

(a) acquire the training and services necessary to support increasingly productive activity;

(b) learn about contraceptives and other family planning measures to free them from unwanted pregnancies;

(c) become literate so that they can learn about techniques, gain information, and explore general areas of knowledge of interest to them;   and

(d) develop and practise leadership skills as an avenue for bringing new knowledge to their villages and representing village interests to government representatives at the thana level.

Training and institution building are key elements in the programme.   Previously there were no village level institutions for reaching out to and working with rural women.   Rural women's isolation means they have had little experience with organisations such as co-operatives and therefore little opportunity to develop leadership skills, savings, credit and production planning.

The project is set up in the following way.   In 25 thanas, i.e. at least one in each of the country's 19 districts, where IRDP is already operating a programme for male farmers, a women's programme has been introduced into the IRDP project.   The project is being developed as part of a total village development scheme involving both rural men and women. It is administered by three female staff members under the authority of an IRDP male project officer. These women are responsible for organising women's co-operatives in the villages. These serve as viable village-based institutions for women.

To become a co-operative member, a village woman must buy a share and accept a discipline spelled out in the by-laws. Women are obliged to make regular weekly savings deposits in the co-operative bank and to attend village meetings. As members they are entitled to credit, training, services and supplies.

Each co-operative must send five members to the thana centre every week for training. These five women are then expected to transmit what they have learned at weekly village meetings to their own co-operative.

So far there has been no serious obstacle to the formation of co-operatives or to the attendance of five women from each co-operative at the thana centre. To date, 364 co-operatives have been formed and attendance at thana training is 80 to 90 per cent.

At the thana centre, the women have new opportunities as a result of the project. A direct result is the weekly training class for women which is provided by government extension officers from various ministries who sit at the thana centre - for example, the education officer, the family planning officer, the co-operatives officer, and so forth. This is probably the first time that most of these extension agents have had access to such numbers of villagers, who are, in fact, the appropriate audience for much of their expertise. Whatever it is that the Government wants to communicate to rural women - including information about family planning - it now has direct access without having to go to individual households.

This training also helps in developing leadership among those responsible rural women in communication, management and administration of the co-operatives. As representatives of rural women, they bring to the attention of the Government the real needs of rural women and make demands to meet those needs. The viability of the co-operatives depends to a great extent on their leadership and its management abilities.

The training programme also provides a chance for these five women from each co-operative to have a sanctioned trip out of the village - perhaps to check market prices, to talk with women from other villages, to have direct access to medical facilities, and other government services. Each co-operative needed 15 members to start with officially. Most co-operatives started with just 15 members and membership remained static during the initial months until the co-operatives could be registered and loans issued. Then the numbers rapidly increased so that now co-operatives that have been in operation for about a year and have given one round of loans have at least 40 members.

About 15,000 co-operative members in 25 thanas have saved about 600,000 takas. Saving is considered an important part of the project both by the administrators and the participants. Women usually give two answers to why they have joined co-operatives - one is for the chance to take loans and the other is to save money for future needs.

Village women attend co-operative meetings in the village for
an hour or two a week.   Part of the meeting is taken up with collection of savings - women who cannot attend often send their weekly
deposit along with someone who can.   Part of the meeting is taken
up with an explanation of what was learned at the thana centre.

One important focus of learning, of course, is the opportunity
for taking loans.   They are taught how to prepare group production
plans which specify what each member plans to do with her loan.
On the basis of this production plan, loan money is given to the
leaders of the co-operative who distribute the loans to the members.
Though the loans are to individuals for individual projects, the
co-operative is responsible for repayment of the loans and is not
eligible for another round of loans until the first ones have been
repaid.

As of December 1977, 1,300,000 takas were given in amounts of
50-300 takas to women in 18 thanas.   A survey was done to see how
women were using loans and it indicates that the largest use of
loans was to buy paddy from the market, process it into rice, and
sell it at a profit.   The second largest use was to invest in
goats, cows and chickens.   A few thanas have already given a series
of loans and no trouble has been reported about repayment.   In some
thanas women are asking for larger loans and longer periods of
repayment.   Much attention is given to the introduction of improved
agricultural technology, such as threshing machines, black polythene
sheets to dry paddy or hand pumps for the irrigation of vegetable
fields.

As a supplemental experiment, selected members from a group of
co-operatives are being sent to various places in Bangladesh for
intensive training in appropriate skills that might provide the
basis for commercial investment.   Ways are being explored to bring
better health services to women.   Commercial poultry raising and
vegetable growing and literacy classes are under experiment in
several thanas.   Family planning has been well received by co-
operative members; about 40 per cent of the co-operative members
have accepted family planning.   The project has without doubt
provided village women with necessary access to the information and
services that the Government has developed.   The results have been
impressive and should be more so as government services improve.

II.   Women's contribution to the rural economy

Any development programmes for rural women should recognise
the full scope of women's activities and problems.   Besides their
reproductive and nurturing roles, rural women in Bangladesh are
also engaged in farm household activities and are making an
important contribution to the rural economy.   They are responsible
for seed storage and preservation, grain storage, post harvest rice
processing, vegetable and fruit growing, poultry raising, livestock
care, fruit processing, food preservation, fuel gathering, household
manufacture, building maintenance and repair.   These activities
are often invisible because women work out of the sight of most men.
The men in the family, in addition, do not like to report that they
cannot afford to provide leisure and luxury for their women,
specially if women are doing jobs which lower their family status.
As a result, rural women's economic contribution is not calculated
in accounting systems for GNP or in records of labour force participation.   Yet in designing any development programmes for rural
women due attention must be given to the actual and potential role
of women in economically productive work.

III. Economic motivation

Development programmes for women should be addressed to the problems that concern rural women. Economic motivation is central to rural women's behaviour. Women need money not only to contribute to the family as a whole but also to save for emergencies and for times when they and their families are in distress. Thus, when a woman is urgently concerned with her family's economic and social security, she may not be interested in acquiring modern knowledge in nutrition or health practices or in literacy classes which, though related to her primary needs, are of secondary importance to her. However, once a certain amount of economic security has been achieved, rural women will be interested in other social changes desired for comprehensive development of the community and society.

IV. Introduction of improved technology and its effect on rural women's productivity

As men are usually the decision makers and their activities are visible in rural societies, there is always a tendency for activities performed by them to be modernised in preference to women's. In most agricultural policies attention is focused on modernisation and improved technologies for crop production which is done by men in the field rather than on post harvest activities which is women's work. Moreover, development efforts to modernise or bring into the cash economy those subsistence level activities traditionally done by women, like rice processing, grain storage or poultry raising tend to go to men and machines. As a result the expert knowledge of women in these areas is lost, and women are being more and more isolated from modern technological progress and confined to a marginal role of unskilled labourers. Women lose work which means loss of status, and the knowledge gap between men and women widens, bringing a social disbalance in the family. If national policy favours keeping rural women in economically productive work, then training and employment of rural women would be required for their effective participation in aspects of "modernised" rural work.

V. Given sufficient and appropriate training, women can plan, implement and monitor development programmes

Education and training, both formal and informal, are important factors influencing the effectiveness of women's participation in rural development. In Bangladesh, rural women constitute the majority of the illiterate population. The vocational and technical training of girls and women is even more neglected than their general education. So far, only their social roles have received some recognition in training programmes especially intended for women. Most of the vocational courses offered to girls and women are, in fact, in such fields as sewing, embroidery, and handicrafts, which have little market value. Handicrafts are produced by women in their homes since they can thus combine such income-earning activities with their other household activities. However, fashions change quickly and competition among thousands of workers usually keeps wages at the minimum level. As such, handicrafts, though providing some employment, have not really improved women's lot. The vocational training of rural women should include use of modern farming tools and techniques which will increase their productivity and lead to economic independence.

Women in rural development:
The People's Republic of China

Elisabeth Croll

It is important to draw attention to the significance of The People's Republic of China in generally considering women both as agents and beneficiaries of the rural development process. China constitutes a significant case study because of the particular form which rural development has taken there, the scope and scale of the attempted redefinition of the role and status of women, and because this process of social change has been monitored and has been the subject of conscious analysis within China for the past 25 years. An examination of the strategies which have been adopted in China provides an opportunity to study a sequence of policies by which one country has, over a period of time, consciously attempted to fulfil some of the commonly recognised preconditions necessary to relate and integrate policies of rural development and policies to redefine the role and status of women.

The strategy adopted in China once the new Government had taken power can be conveniently divided into four differing policy categories. The first group of policies assigned a new legal status to women as a result of the new legislation which provided for the equality and protection of women and children. What is important to note is that the promulgation of the marriage, labour and land laws was followed by extensive campaigns to make the new legal provisions and facilities widely known and available throughout the country. The second group of policies encouraged women to enter fully into social production and political activities. In the tradition of Marx and Engels, the Chinese Communist Party has always assumed entry into social production to be a necessary condition for the emancipation of women and to be a direct correlation between it and the distribution of power and authority accruing to women in the domestic and public domains. During the successive government policies to increase production and to replace individualised peasant production by collectivised agriculture and the establishment of rural industries and projects of capital construction, measures have been introduced to particularly encourage women to take a full and wide-ranging part in social production. These included the establishment of separate work teams for women, training courses, the principle of equal remuneration for equal work, labour protection measures, and programmes to reduce the individual household responsibilities of women.

The third group of policies was designed to establish a new ruling ideology incorporating new definitions of women to replace male supremacy and female subordination, secondariness and dependence. To eradicate the traditional ruling ideology of Confucianism, the Government encouraged a number of educational and conscience-raising programmes, language reforms and rewriting of educational texts to identify and criticise the remaining influences of the now out-moded code of ethics, proverbs and folk-lore. The fourth group of policies was to do with the separate organisations of women which were established on the grounds that women had a special experience of oppression different from that of men and the necessity to form an independent power base from which women could conduct their own struggle to negotiate new rights and opportunities. Local groups of women were

first established in the villages of rural China as part of the
nation-wide construction of the women's movement and they have
played a key role in implementing the new policies and raising the
individual and collective confidence of peasant women.

A different question is the degree to which this four-pronged
strategy had been successful in achieving its goals. Women in
China have indeed benefited from the rural development process.
They have certainly entered into new economic and political roles
which were hitherto male preserves. The value attached to their
labour power has visibly increased and women have attended classes
aimed at increasing their levels of education and technical skills
in order to reduce the gender-related division of labour within
the work force. Many facilities have been provided to improve
their health and accommodate their reproductive roles, but at the
same time, women in the non-professional sectors of the economy
still tend to be found predominantly among the less skilled and
lower-paid members of the work force. In politics, women's very
participation was innovatory, but they were still likely to
constitute only 20 to 30 per cent of the representatives or
leadership groups, a figure well below their proportion represented
in the population or in social production. The services to reduce
the household responsibilities of women have been very unevenly
implemented, and within the domestic sphere the individual household still functions as a unit of production in rural areas; this
self-provisioning, transformation and consumption of foods, the
minor allocation of resources to community services, and the
division of labour within the household places women at a
disadvantage in the public domain. The traditional customs of
surname exogamy and patrilocal marriage continues to cause a
preference for male children and the elaboration of male kinship
groups. For much of their lives, then, women still remain
"temporary" or "outside" members of their households in rural
areas. Despite a high commitment to improving the position of
women in China, some problems have continued to inhibit further
redefinitions of their position.

An assessment of the policies themselves in redefining the
position of women is therefore necessary. Three problem areas
can be singled out for further discussion. Firstly the wide-scale
entry of women into social production in China in the 1950s had
shown that this might be a necessary, but certainly not a sufficient,
condition in bringing about changes in the position of women.
Changes in the economic base or qualitative transformations in the
mode of production and the establishment of new social institutions
did not necessarily mean the creation of new norms determining
social behaviour. In the 1960s and 1970s ideological constraints
have been identified in China as the main forces hindering
improvement in the position of women and it is their removal
which has proved to be a particularly necessary and arduous area
of struggle in working for social change. The second problem
area has to do with the continuing exchange of women in marriage
between patrilocal households and kin groups and the function of
both of these in the economy. Many socio-economic functions
still accrue to individual rural households and these demand that
it continue to mobilise its resources in order to find solutions
to a number of organisational problems, namely production and the
transformation of materials for consumption. The combined
demands of each of the three sectors of the rural economy,
collective, private and domestic, relies on the distribution of

the labour resources of the household between the three sectors and especially on the unpaid labour of women. Many of the policies to redefine the position of women have in fact been modified in rural areas in the interests of servicing and maintaining the household as a unit of production and consumption. The third problem area concerns the role of the separate organisations of women in defending the interests of women within the development process. Their very presence in rural villages in itself marked a redefinition in the position of women, but their history has also been marked by certain ambiguities which surround their position as an independent power base in a society in which class consciousness and class struggle are viewed as the motivating forces generating social change. The Government has always demanded of the women's groups that in addition to improving their own status, they also respond to all forms of class oppression, but the uneasy alliance between the revolutionary and women's movements has sometimes brought competing claims on the identity of women and the balance of their dual demands has directly affected the ability of local groups to defend the interests of its members. Various factors which have affected the history of women's groups in rural China can be highlighted and recent events in China which have been responsible for assigning a new value to women's groups can be outlined.

Our over-all aim is not to necessarily advocate the experience of China as a single model for emulation, but to identify the areas where changes in the position of women have indeed been introduced and to identify the problem areas which have characterised one of the most comprehensive and integrated attempts to redefine the role and status of rural women.[1]

---

[1] More extended bibliography on the subject can be found in E. Croll, Women and Rural Development: The People's Republic of China, ILO, Geneva, 1979.

Rural women and the social organisation
of production - some conceptual issues

Gita Sen

There is an increasing understanding among development
economists of the importance of situating the problems of rural
people within a general context of social relations and systemic
change. In part, this understanding has been fuelled by the inability
of most rural co-operation schemes to improve the living standards
of the poorer sections of the population or to solve very basic
survival problems. We see fairly clearly that different sections/
social classes in the rural area have different problems and
often conflicting interests - policies devised without taking
this into account usually end up benefiting the economically
stronger strata at the expense of the weaker. This paper is
premised on the view that the problems of rural women must be
analysed from this perspective.

Empirically, there is substantial variation across social
classes and regions of the world in the ways in which rural women
appear to be integrated into the system of social production.
However there is also an empirical commonality in the involvement
of poorer women in similar ways in subsistence production
activities - they gather fuel, fetch water, process and prepare
food - in addition to engaging in wage labour or petty trade.
In coming to grips with both the variation and the commonality,
three conceptual issues must be clarified. This paper attempts
to explore these issues in some depth.

The first concern is to avoid the positivist pitfall of
equating the simple empirical categories with conceptual categories.
In order to accomplish this, we have to question the significance
of both the subsistence activities and the position of rural women
within the system of social production. To do this we pose the
following questions:

(1) What is the relation between the accumulation of capital and
subsistence production activities in the rural area?

(2) Given these relations, how do we understand the specific
position of rural women? In what way can we distinguish it from
the position of rural men?[1] What are the similarities?

(3) What conflicts are involved in the position of the rural
woman? What forms of action and programmes can alter her
oppression?

The answer to the first question must begin by acknowledging
that within the system of capitalist production, the survival of
particular workers is entirely contingent on the vagaries of the
demand for labour. When workers (and members of the working
class in general) are able to obtain an adequate subsistence, that
is the result of the working out of a number of forces - the labour
requirements of capital, the existing pool of unemployed, and the
level of organisation of the workers themselves. Thus while a
labour force is necessary for surplus extraction, no particular
group of workers is guaranteed their subsistence a priori. All

---

[1] Our focus is on the problems of the rural poor.

forms of subsistence activity undertaken by workers who are
in the process of separation from the means of subsistence through
mechanisms of social differentiation in the countryside must be
viewed in this light as struggles for survival. The greater the
pressure on the means of subsistence of the rural poor, the more
arduous and difficult the activity of providing for their subsistence
becomes - the labour intensity of the activity tends to increase
along with the precariousness of survival. For the rural poor in
the Third World today, survival is a daily question, and almost
all activities are subsistence activities. There is little
question of accumulation here. Everything from foraging, gathering,
and the production of food on available land to petty trade,
production of market crops and hiring out as wage or bonded
labour bears the stamp of subsistence activity. Subsistence
production is not defined by the nature of the work involved but
by the performer's relationship to the means of subsistence. Both
women and men from the households of the rural poor engage
in subsistence activity in this social sense. What then
differentiates the women from the men?

        Empirically we know that there is usually a fairly sharp
sexual division of labour defining and distinguishing the tasks
performed by women from those done by men. This applies both to
domestic work and to wider activity relating to production and
trade outside the home. Minimally, two features distinguish the
work done by women: whatever other kinds of work (wage labour,
trade) women may do, they tend to be responsible for all the
domestic labour centred around food preparation, and of course,
child bearing; this usually means that women work much longer
hours than men do over-all.

        In attempting to explain this division of labour, there is
a temptation to see the interests of men and women as simply
opposed, or at least mutually exclusive. This presupposes a
form of sexual individuation of persons in society which is
rather problematic. Both women and men exist socially not as
simple individuals but through their relationship to households.
It is within the household that the mechanisms of survival and
subsistence are organised - these range from the sexual and age-
wise division of labour, and forms of production activity, to
fertility and other decisions affecting biological reproduction.
These mechanisms are usually bound together by sets of authority
relations, e.g., patriarchy, that imply dominance and
subordination. This is not therefore a consensual model of the
household. Nor is the household a static structure, but one that
changes as people adapt to changing social conditions of
survival brought about by social differentiation. What is important
is to see rural women through the lens of the rural households
to which they are connected - without this, one can end up with
very misleading pictures of the range of decision making and
autonomy open to them. Even when they exist as single women with
no apparent empirical connection to a larger household, we
can understand their situation only by examining the reasons for
their singleness, rather than by assuming it as given. What is
common to both women and men is their survival through their
connection to households; what is distinct is the nature of
the connection.

More specifically, in answer to our third question, the place of the women is a contradictory one, fraught with conflict. The survival of the household as a whole and with it her own survival is often obtained at the particular expense of the woman. For example, it may be imperative to the household's ability to make debt repayments that there be a large number of children who can be sent out as wage labour - it is the woman of course who bears the physical hardship and danger of childbirth, often with little say in the matter; but as a member of the household, her own subsistence is closely bound up with survival of the household. Similar conflicts may be seen in the performance of domestic husbanding which may involve enormous time and labour. This is not to deny the gain to male household members from the women's double day. It is rather to see that the woman's own survival may be contingent upon how well those tasks are performed.

Social programmes of action must take this contradictory position of women into account - schemes for rural action which bring poor rural women together to pool and rationalise work activity are most likely to be useful, e.g., the provision of technology and resources to make co-operation in food processing possible will both reduce individual effort and not endanger the survival of the household. Similarly the provision of adequate medical facilities will make childbearing less dangerous and by reducing infant mortality, reduce the number of pregnancies, again without affecting adversely the conditions of people's survival. Short of a drastic change in the social system, these types of measures which not only distinguish women by social class but fully acknowledge their contradictory position are the only ones likely to ameliorate the lot of rural women.

III. GENERAL DISCUSSION

What follows is a summary of some of the most important topics covered in the discussion:

1. Modes of production, agrarian structures and women's work

Discussion in this session covered a number of issues fairly widely.

Firstly, it was felt that it is important to know more about the relationship between hierarchical versus egalitarian productive structures and women's position within them. In other words, should we expect that more egalitarian productive structures will automatically result in greater equality between the sexes? Or is a change in the mode of production, say from a capitalist to a socialist mode, necessary and sufficient to ensure this equality? It was generally felt that socialist forms might tend to facilitate women's access to productive resources by eliminating inequalities between men and women that are derived from their different access to property rights. However, there was a general agreement on the insufficiency of this change if it is not accompanied by measures aimed at freeing women from domestic chores and reorganising the division of labour between the sexes. Examples from countries undergoing processes of change towards some form of socialist structures reinforced this position. What can be observed is a continuation of forms of subordination parallel to those observed in other countries, such as the marginalisation of rural women in the less remunerative and less modernised subsectors in agriculture. It is necessary that these changes be accompanied by a continuous surveillance of the process from the point of view of eliminating factors that make possible the maintenance of women's subordinate position in rural societies.

In societies where private property predominates, different forms of ownership imply different access of women to productive resources. A basic question is whether women have the same rights to own land as men do and, if so, whether their rights are de facto upheld. The access to ownership of land is limited for women in many societies due, for example, to inheritance systems that follow a patrilineal pattern. Yet there are many cases in which women's property rights are recognised by law or tradition, although in practice they are hardly functional. In this sense, contradictions might develop between the sexual equality recognised by the law and the inequality that appears in its implementation.

These problems are compounded in situations where a basic economic transformation is being carried out without other fundamental changes. In the case of the Ethiopian land reform, for example, it was pointed out that the recognition of similar rights for women in their access to land cannot be very meaningful in practice without other fundamental changes in family laws - since men are the head of the household by constitutional right. In the same way, the allocation of land to families when households are polygamous is bound not to respond adequately to the needs of individual women within the household. That is, the family is not an adequate unit in that case.

The issue of what constitutes an ideal land reform from the point of view of women was discussed. At the general level, women will be affected by land reform - like other individuals - according to their class background. Land reforms in this respect, will be judged according to the degree of redistribution carried out, its technical aspects, parallel services created, etc. However, from the point of view of women's interests, there is an extra dimension which has often been neglected and that is the establishment of equal accessibility to land regardless of sex. The recognition of this extra dimension carries with it a great deal of policy implications and suggestions for action which must be made concrete in each specific case.

A different issue that affects women is their accessibility to labour and the control over the labour process and its outcome, that is, the control over output. Men often have greater access to labour inputs than women do and greater control over the proceeds obtained. It is, therefore, insufficient to look into the question of equality of access to land; access to labour and the control over output also need to be taken into consideration. In order to best understand these questions in each case, it is necessary to analyse each mode of production with the specificity of regions and local rural communities. This calls for in-depth studies to understand these processes and the dynamics of change that lead to them.

Rural women tend to lag much behind men in matters concerning education and training. Illiteracy rates are higher among women, and it is well known that training related to the introduction of new technology tends to be given to men - relegating women to the traditional, less productive tasks. There are even absurd cases in which training courses have been given to men for tasks performed exclusively by women - therefore setting the basis for the expulsion of women from their traditional area of work. Policies geared towards increasing women's access to and attendance at school and training programmes should therefore be recommended and insisted upon.

Finally, in matters of rural policy, it is important to differentiate between the individual and the family, since it cannot be assumed that all members benefit equally from family resources. In addition, more work is necessary to conceptualise the household; what do we mean by it and how does the concept apply to different family structures? How do the dynamics of change in agrarian structures affect the household and how does it affect each member? It is clear that the assumption made so often by researchers and policy makers that the household is a basic unit of production and consumption, must be called into question since it does not take into consideration the internal inequalities between individual members.

2. Sex roles and the division
   of labour in rural economies

A basic question discussed in this session was the under-estimation of women's economic activities. Survey studies show that women's work in agriculture is severely under-rated due to a variety of reasons, while domestic work containing a high degree of production for the family's own consumption is never counted as an economic activity. Statistical data gathering needs to be improved along these lines.

It is clear that, although the concentration of women in domestic work is almost universal, there are great variations in the sexual division of labour in non-domestic activities. We need to study with greater depth the nature and factors affecting the sexual division of labour, what types of jobs women perform and why, and the reasons for the great variations that can be observed. In particular, we need to ask whether we can talk of "patterns" in the division of labour by sex and what significance and implications they have at the theoretical and practical level. The importance of women's self-perception was also emphasised as a factor influencing their role in rural economies.

A positive correlation between women's participation in non-domestic production and their role in decision making has been observed. However, this does not necessarily imply that whenever women's participation in non-domestic work increases there is a parallel improvement in their status, since the increase in decision making tends to take place within the realm of so-called secondary activities. Therefore, the problem here is to design programmes and action that open all kinds of activities to rural women.

In our analysis of women's roles and the sexual division of labour it is important to focus on the dynamics of change and how this often not only generates a new division of labour between the sexes but also creates new forms of subordination for women. Without a clear understanding of this dynamic, policies affecting women may fall short of dealing comprehensively with the conditions that affect the attainment of equality between the sexes. For example, it is far from clear that wage labour "liberates" women. To be sure, it might provide a source of financial independence, but to the extent that women are exploited and subject to wage and other types of discrimination it represents the creation of a new form of subordination which must be understood as such.

A great interest in methodological questions led to a discussion on this subject. It was agreed that there are important theoretical gaps in analysis. For example, any methodology that does not incorporate power relationships between classes and sexes is bound to be inadequate in analyses concerning women. Another question posed was how to get information about women's work. The problems of a once-and-for-all survey and particularly of time allocation studies was discussed. It was agreed that what is important is to capture tendencies and processes of dynamic change - an objective that cannot be achieved with time allocation studies. In rural areas, a one-day observation, even if dealing with a very large sample, can lead to very misleading conclusions. It is important to know who is doing what - and this may vary depending upon household, day and season. The number of minutes invested in different tasks are not sufficient to capture factors such as the dynamics of subordination and decision-making factors which are essential to understand fully the nature of women's work. Interviews and participatory observation methods of research may be the most reliable.

Rural women can be found among the poorest of the poor. It was pointed out that if one wants to mobilise the poor, and women among them, one must be clear about the concept of mobilisation. Action needs to be based on knowledge, and it requires a great effort to increase consciousness. A starting point for action should be a clear understanding of the most immediate contradictions that people face rather than any a priori ideological position.

It is for this reason, i.e. the emphasis placed on ideology in a one-dimensional way, that political parties have so often neglected women's issues.

3. Effects of the penetration of the market on women's work

The penetration of capitalism into subsistence economies has affected women in a variety of ways. There is a lot of evidence to show that a good proportion of these effects are negative. This does not imply that one should assume that negative effects are always the general rule; the specificity of each case needs to be analysed. In the case of Ghana examined, the penetration of the market generated: (a) an increase in women's workload; (b) the relegation of women to the food/subsistence sector and the migration of men or their concentration in commercial crop produc-tion; (c) an increase in female-headed households; and (d) the shift from more to less nutritious food production due to the need to economise labour. The discussion centred around the difficulty to find a solution to this type of situation which creates a vicious circle of inter-related problems. Piecemeal measures are bound to fail since what is necessary is to break that vicious circle, and this requires a global approach in order to change basic economic relationships.

In the case of India, capitalist penetration has eroded the basis of subsistence. This is at the root of the process of pauperisation found among peasants. The marginalisation of women is greater than that of men because men are absorbed more easily into the wage labour force. In addition, capitalist penetration has also meant for women the loss of control over their own produc-tion in the area of small crafts - a process by which they become exploited by those who commercialise their products. Here too , the solution calls for far-reaching changes in land distribution and employment creation. If less far-reaching solutions are considered, it is important to be clear about the fact that some of them - such as the training and placement of women in typically "female jobs" - are bound to perpetuate or create new forms of sub-ordination.

Regional differences in Colombia were discussed from the point of view of how women's work and functions are linked with national and international markets. The information presented was also seen as an illustration of the usefulness of analysing historical processes of change in agrarian structures and the gradual penetra-tion of the market from the perspective of understanding the position of women within them. More specifically, it was agreed that an historical perspective is useful for analysing and understanding changes in the sexual division of labour since it makes possible a dynamic type of analysis.

The use of women as reserve labour was also discussed. When male labour is not available, women are drawn into the labour force, very often under more unstable conditions and lower pay than men. Yet this does not release them from total responsibility for the care of children and family maintenance - a feature that is over-whelming across countries and regions. Women, therefore, provide a cheap and extremely flexible reserve of labour since, when they are not needed, they can always fall back on their domestic acti-vities. The implications of this fact for the employment of women needs to be analysed further.

4.   Rural development and women

There is still a need to deal further with the question of whether rural women have fared badly from the process of development and if so, why. In particular one needs to study the mechanisms by which the process of development affects women. Differentiation must be made between the various approaches to development in order to analyse the role played by women in each case. In some cases, a contradictory situation may arise because the position of women might both improve and deteriorate at the same time, depending upon what aspects of their situation one is looking at.

Criticisms of the concept of "integration of women in development" were voiced. What does the concept mean? The term is based on the assumption that women are housewives and do not participate in production. For the most part this is not the case for rural women and in any case, women always play an essential role in the development process. The question is what is that role and how is it "integrated" within that process since it can be performed under many forms of patriarchal subordination and oppression. The current usage of the concept need imply nothing more than the participation of women in a process which generates new forms of subordination for them. In addition, the concept of integration implies that one should aspire for women whatever men get from the development process - an implication which is highly questionable.

More research is needed about the different ways by which capitalist enterprises make use of traditional social relations and introduce them into capitalist production. In Morocco, for example, the craft sector has been moved from the house to the factory and women are employed and brought in with children. In the same way, women work under the umbrella of their husbands in agro-business employment - such as in the tomato production geared to the European market. This marriage between the old and the new can result in very exploitative conditions for women.

In the development literature, the household is often assumed to be a static unit of production and consumption. As pointed out earlier, it is also viewed as a unit without differentiating between individual members in terms of access to resources and roles played. Yet the household is subject to a constant process of transformation due to the effects that outside factors have upon the household's access to resources, individual members' roles, fertility rates, household production, etc. There are also several types of households - polygamous, extended family, individual family, female-headed units, etc. - which need to be differentiated. The importance of focusing on the household comes from the central role that it plays in determining women's activities and their condition. The analysis of its dynamics and of the role of each individual within it is fundamental for an understanding of the problems facing women.

The question of "what kind of development for women" is a very complex one since it must be parallel, not subordinate to the wider question of "what kind of development for people". Very often the questions are viewed as being incompatible, at least at the initial stages in which the satisfaction of essential needs is of primary urgency. Yet it is often at these stages when sexual inequalities are introduced and must be prevented. The two questions are not incompatible but parallel.

Along these lines, the discussion centred around "reformist"
versus "radical" change - as in the case studies of Bangladesh and
China presented at the meeting. It was agreed that, to the extent
that radical change may reduce exploitation and hierarchical forms
of organisation, the possibility to do away with different forms
of subordination increases. Yet it may not be a sufficient condition either because some degree of exploitation and hierarchy may
still persist or/and because the household, and the role of women
in it, is left intact. The case of China was seen as an illustration of a country that has made an important effort to improve the
condition of women, but problems of inequality still persist; the
emergence of old and new problems and resistance to change points
to the need for a continuous effort not only to move ahead but also
to prevent deterioration. On the other hand, when only "reformist"
reforms are possible, the scope for change is more limited. Yet
a project such as that of Bangladesh can raise a number of questions
and introduce some change at the local level. It also raises a
series of contradictions - between the goals set up by the projects
and their actual implementation - that are likely to become a
dynamic force for future change.

IV. CONCLUSIONS

1. Programmes on women

The importance of setting up special women's programmes was stressed, given the past neglect of women's issues in research programmes and in development literature. As one speaker put it, "so far we have had history; now we need her story". Women's invisibility and silence must be replaced by a continuous effort to stress and explain the essential role played by women at all levels. This continuous effort, as another speaker put it, should not mislead us "in not stressing the obvious".

The importance of research, as a pre-requisite for action, was also emphasised repeatedly. Without a clear analysis of the essential problems facing women. policy and action are bound to be incomplete at best and perhaps seriously harmful. It was suggested that an important objective of research should be to define the direction and the guidelines for what should be done, i.e. to define goals more sharply. More concrete action should follow from this, depending upon possibilities for implementation.

2. Research priorities

The discussion on research priorities centred around three levels:

(a) Studies concentrating on a specific topic. These would include country studies and in-depth research focusing on a specific area of interest. The following were among the topics that were singled out as needing special attention at the present time:

- the effects of the penetration of the market on rural women's work;

- means of control of labour in agrarian production systems;

- legal and other de facto handicaps to rural women's control over productive resources;

- the seasonality and part-time nature of women's work and its consequences;

- women as agricultural wage workers and the nature of wage discrimination;

- the role of traditional women's organisations in the past and their projection into the future;

- the under-estimation of women's economic activities at the domestic level as well as outside of the household;

- women's reactions against oppression: concrete case studies.

(b) Synthesis work. The objective in this case is to draw empirical research together with the purpose of arriving at higher levels of generalisation regarding the significance of empirical findings for policy, action and conceptual work. It was agreed that, given the increasing amount of empirical research being carried out at present, synthesis work is becoming progressively more necessary. In addition to the synthesis derived from the topics listed above, the following are other illustrations of this type of research:

   - the nature of the household economy in agricultural societies;

   - what is a "good" agrarian reform from the point of view of rural women's interests;

   - women's experiences in self-management;

   - discovering patterns affecting the sexual division of labour - if necessary, how can it be changed?

   - rural women and development: to what degree is there a process of marginalisation of women?

(c) Regional and cross-country comparisons. Although this type of research can also be considered as synthesising, the emphasis in this case should be on appraising differences and similarities between countries and regions, and between different development processes. Comparisons can be drawn for example along the lines of the topics and areas of interest outlined above.

3. Other practical recommendations

Five areas were pointed out as having particular importance and needing increasing attention:

(a) education and training;

(b) employment creation;

(c) discrimination in wages and other aspects of wage employment;

(d) social security measures for rural women;

(e) basic needs and women.

First, in the area of education and training, emphasis should be placed on achieving equal access of men and women to all types of skills in order to avoid sexual segregation and dualism. Second, the need for projects of employment creation to which women have equal access is of primary importance given the marginalisation to which women have been subjected in many countries. Third, measures must be taken to end all practices of discrimination which result in lower wages for women and the payment of women's and children's work to male heads of households. Fourth, social security measures and social services for rural women must be studied and recommended. Not only is

there a great lag between urban and rural standards along these
lines; the gap must be bridged but, in addition, the different
needs of the two cases must be spelled out in order to implement
the necessary measures.   Finally, work on basic needs must take
into consideration the implications of this strategy for women
and their role within it.